An Introduction to the Law of the European Economic Community

edited by

B. A. WORTLEY

O.B.E., Q.C., LL.D.

MANCHESTER UNIVERSITY PRESS

U.S.A.: OCEANA PUBLICATIONS INC

Published by the University of Manchester at
THE UNIVERSITY PRESS
316–324 Oxford Road, Manchester M13 9NR
UK ISBN 0 7190 0481 0

U.S.A.
OCEANA PUBLICATIONS INC
75 Main Street, Dobbs Ferry, N.Y. 10522

Distributed in India by
N. M. TRIPATHI (PRIVATE) LTD
Princess Street, Bombay 2

Library of Congress Cataloging in Publication data

Main entry under title: *An introduction to the law of the European Economic Community*

(The Melland Schill lectures)
Includes bibliographical references.
CONTENTS: General introduction, by B. A. Wortley.—The Common Market: the geographical and general background, by G. North.—Preparing the authentic text of the E.E.C. treaty, by M. Akehurst.—Company law and the Common Market: the first step, by J. A. Emlyn Davies.—The Court of Justice of the European Communities, by G. White.—Monopolies under the E.E.C. treaty, by B. A. Wortley.—Restrictive practices under the E.E.C. treaty, by B. A. Wortley.—Appendices.
1. Law—European Economic Community countries—Addresses, essays, lectures. 2. International and municipal law—Gt. Brit.—Addresses, essays, lectures. I. Wortley, Ben Atkinson, 1907– , ed. II. Series.

LAW 340′.094 72–39410
US ISBN 0 379 11912 9

Printed in Great Britain by
Butler & Tanner Ltd, Frome and London

AN INTRODUCTION TO THE LAW OF THE EUROPEAN ECONOMIC COMMUNITY

THE MELLAND SCHILL LECTURES
delivered at the University of Manchester
and published by the University Press

The Law of International Institutions in Europe
by A. H. Robertson, B.C.L., S.J.D., 1961
The Role of International Law in the Elimination of War
by Professor Quincy Wright, 1961
The Acquisition of Territory in International Law
by Professor R. Y. Jennings, 1962
The Sources and Evidences of International Law
by Clive Parry, LL.D., 1965
Rights in Air Space
by D. H. N. Johnson, M.A., LL.B., 1965
International Law and the Practitioner
by Sir Francis A. Vallat, K.C.M.G., Q.C., 1966
The Law of the Sea
by D. W. Bowett, M.A., LL.B., Ph.D., 1967
International Law and the Uses of Outer Space
by J. E. S. Fawcett, M.A., 1968
Modern Diplomatic Law
by M. Hardy, M.A., LL.M., 1968
The United Nations in a Changing World
by J. A. C. Gutteridge, M.A., 1970
Economic World Order?
by Professor Georg Schwarzenberger, 1970

OTHER BOOKS ON INTERNATIONAL LAW
Self-defence in International Law
by D. W. Bowett, M.A., LL.B., Ph.D.
Human Rights in Europe
by A. H. Robertson, B.C.L., S.J.D.
The Legal Problems of Foreign Investment in Developing Countries
by E. I. Nwogugu, LL.B., Ph.D.
Human Rights in National and International Law
edited by A. H. Robertson, B.C.L., S.J.D.
Legal Aspects of Foreign Investment in the European Economic Community
by W. H. Balekjian, Dr rer. pol., Dr Jur., Ph.D.
The Settlement of Boundary Disputes in International Law
by A. O. Cukwurah, B.C.L., LL.B., Ph.D.
East European Rules on the Validity of International Commercial Arbitration Agreements
by L. Kos-Rabcewicz-Zubkowski, LL.D.
The Codification of Public International Law
by R. P. Dhokalia
Extradition in International Law
by I. A. Shearer, LL.M., S.J.D.
Human Rights in the World
by A. H. Robertson, B.C.L., S.J.D.

CONTENTS

FOREWORD

After arduous negotiations Her Majesty's Government has now signed the treaties of the European Communities. The present work includes the explanatory Government White Paper of May 1967 (Appendix 1), the Directive on Companies (Appendix 2) and Regulation No. 17 on competition (Appendix 3). The first three chapters deal with general background problems and the rest concentrate on matters affecting business dealings.

The views expressed are personal to each individual author and in no sense collective or official.

It is hoped that the book will be a useful introduction for legal practitioners, businessmen and university students.

I should like to thank Dr Gillian White for compiling the index and helping in the preparation of the manuscript, my friend Reginald Pilkington, O.B.E., LL.M., for his work on the proofs, and my son, Richard J. A. Wortley, LL.B., for preparing the list of articles of the E.E.C. Treaty cited in the text, and not least Mr T. L. Jones, Secretary of the Press, and his Assistant, Mr R. H. Offord, for their help in speeding the production of the book.

January 1972

B. A. Wortley
Faculty of Law
University of Manchester

Chapter I

GENERAL INTRODUCTION

B. A. Wortley

This series of six lectures on Common Market law forms the twelfth volume in the series of Melland Schill lectures.[1] This series was provided for by the will of Miss Olive Schill, of Prestbury, to commemorate her brother, Melland, who, though of German family origins, was killed when fighting in the British army in the First World War. Miss Schill's was a vision of a Europe and a world united by law and not by the arbitrary exercise of power—economic, legal or political.

The study of Common Market law is now an essential one for lawyers, and it is essential whether Britain joins the Common Market, i.e. the European Economic Community, now,[2] in the more distant future or never at all. The Common Market is a *fait accompli* and lawyers must be prepared to advise their clients on investments[3] and on commercial transactions with customers in the Common Market, especially in their private international law aspects. If and when this country joins the Market, there will be a direct impact of Market law on our own commercial and industrial law.[4]

We are indeed fortunate in having an excellent introduction to our subject in the White Paper first published by the government in May 1967 as Command paper Cmnd. 3301 and which is reproduced in Appendix 1 to this volume with the permission of the Controller of H.M. Stationery Office.

To this Command paper we direct the attention of all those embarking upon the study of the Common Market. Changes in detail may have taken place since then and there will be many transitional arrangements should the United Kingdom become a member of the E.E.C. However, the position of the Command paper was clearly expressed in Hansard on 19 April 1971 as follows:

TREATY OF ROME

30. MR MOLLOY asked the Attorney-General if he will now consider the publication of a White Paper setting out the constitutional and

legal implications for Great Britain involved in signing the Treaty of Rome.

THE ATTORNEY-GENERAL: No. These implications were fully described in a White Paper published in May 1967. There have been developments in the European Communities since then but these were implicit in the situation as it existed in 1967. Nothing has happened since then to invalidate the broad conclusions reached in the White Paper.[5]

However, until this country is a full member of the Common Market, the main interest will be for those lawyers who handle international commercial transactions. If and when we join the Market, its problems will be of more general interest to lawyers whose clients operate mainly in this country. The chapters which follow are not concerned directly with the special problems of the European Coal and Steel Community nor with Euratom.

The European Economic Community, or the Common Market, now consists of some 200 million customers. It is an elaborate legal structure designed to benefit those customers, despite differences in their legal geography and in their administrative and linguistic traditions. Legal machinery has been set up to support this economic and political venture, and this is now working.

Rudolf Graupner, in *The Rules of Competition in the European Economic Community* (Nijhoff, 1965, at p. 141), sums up the legal machinery when he says:

> . . . legislation in respect of Community law is carried out by the Council of Ministers (which is the federal organ)[6] and the Commission (which is the Executive). The Assembly, which is now the European Parliament, has only consultative (and certain controlling) functions. The Court of Justice is designed to ensure the observance of the Treaty.[7]

Observance of the Common Market Treaty and legislation based thereon is required of member States, of enterprises, and of the Commission itself.[8]

Member States are bound by treaties operating under public international law. To give any single State a veto in respect of all or any actions of the Community would be to make the Treaty illusory (see my letter to *The Times* of 31 July 1971). However, as Dr Bowett points out, the majority voting provisions have, legally or illegally, not by any means always been observed since January 1966.[9]

Any deliberate failure by a member State to observe a treaty is illegal under international law and may result in retorsion or reprisals.[10] Treaties requiring the expenditure of money by us or the revision of our own laws need our legislation and it is not in general the British practice to ratify treaties until the necessary money is forthcoming and any necessary changes in law have been provided for by Parliament.[11] The effect of a treaty on local law varies from country to country, as Mr E. Wall has shown.[12] But the problem of establishing a generally understood meaning of the E.E.C. Treaty is common to all member States. It is dealt with in Chapter III by Dr Michael Akehurst, barrister, formerly of the Faculty of Law of the University of Manchester, now of the University of Keele. A typical problem which will occur if we join is that of modifying our company law to meet the requirements of the E.E.C. Treaty. This is dealt with by Mr Emlyn Davies, B.A., barrister, Principal Assistant Solicitor of the Department of Trade and Industry, in Chapter IV.

Dr Gillian White, barrister, of the Faculty of Law of the University of Manchester, deals with the function of the European Court of Justice and its relations with the courts of member States of the E.E.C. Incidentally, we have the full set of Common Market law reports and all the official publications of and much of the literature on the Common Market in the University Library at Manchester.

When the European Court has already interpreted a provision of the E.E.C. Treaty, any national court thereafter faced with an identical problem may follow it and is not required to refer the point to the European Court under Article 117 so long as the national court is merely applying the European Court's interpretation.[13]

The object of the Court and of the other legal machinery under the Common Market Treaty is, basically, to try to provide for what Aristotle called distributive justice.[14] This is done by encouraging competition in the interests of the consumer.[15]

I shall myself, in Chapters VI and VII, be dealing with legal problems arising out of the Treaty provisions on competition, monopolies and restrictive practices.[16] Most member countries have their own legislation on these matters, but any unfair competition, monopolies or restrictive practices in any single country of the E.E.C. is less serious than it would be if allowed to operate in the whole Market area of 200 million cusomers.[17]

By Article 2 of the E.E.C. Treaty, one of the aims of the

Community is an accelerated raising of the standard of living in the whole Market area; this is to be brought about by competition. The rules of the Market are aimed at making competition fair and free from distortion, so that, in the end, there will be in the Common Market countries the sort of large, free market which obtains today in the United States, in which there are no customs or quota barriers between member states, and in which competition is regulated with the object of protecting the consumer. Like the U.S.A., the E.E.C. is protected by a *common external tariff*, a feature lacking in E.F.T.A.

The modern trend in the free world is towards reducing tariffs —witness the Kennedy round and the work of G.A.T.T.—but there is also a general movement towards large economic groups. Besides the U.S.A., the E.E.C. and E.F.T.A., there are two other large economic groups: China and the COMECON group of non-Chinese communists.[18]

The common law, as modified by the Uniform Commercial Code, dominates in the U.S.A. Soviet-type law governs in COMECON countries.[19] In China the law is still probably in a revolutionary phase. Chinese laws and economic arrangements are largely closed to the outside world; they are State secrets.[20]

The world is divided broadly into two economic groups, that ruled by a market economy and that ruled by a planned economy.[21] Common Market countries are still basically places where considerable liberty in price-fixing remains.[22]

In the E.E.C. the legal systems are 'continental', largely of the Roman law family. On the one hand, the Napoleonic tradition of France was widely imitated in Belgium, Luxembourg, Holland and Italy. The German codes, which followed the unification of the State in 1871, are somewhat longer and more modern.[23]

So much for legal geography.[24] Suffice it to say that continued efforts are being made to unify the commercial laws of the world inside[25] and outside the E.E.C., but, despite these efforts, not least those of the International Institute for the Unification of Private Law,[26] and now those of U.N.C.T.A.D., much remains to be done.

In order, however, to understand the factual situation in which we now find ourselves in Western Europe, Mr Geoffrey North, Senior Lecturer in Geography in the University of Manchester, has provided the background chapter (Chapter II). Breaking new ground, this sets the scene by describing the geographical and general background of the Common Market countries.

NOTES

[1] See p. vii above.

[2] See *U.K. and European Communities,* Cmnd. 4715, 8 July 1971.

[3] See Balekjian, *Legal Aspects of Foreign Investment in the European Economic Community,* Manchester, 1967.

[4] See *Legal and Constitutional Implications of U.K. Membership of the European Communities,* 1967, Cmnd. 3301, which deals not only with the Common Market but also Euratom and the European Coal and Steel Community and is set out in Appendix 1 of the present volume

[5] Hansard (Commons), 19 April 1971 (written), col. 337.

[6] An important directive issued by the Council on company matters is discussed in Chapter II and reprinted in Appendix 2.

[7] See Chapter IV, by G. White.

[8] For a fuller account, see Cmnd. 3301, pp. 3–7.

[9] See his *Law of International Institutions,* second edition, 1970, p. 188; also Zaring, *Decision for Europe,* Baltimore, Md., 1969, p. 94.

[10] Dr White deals with the legal remedies of and against the Commission of the Community and of and against States before the Court of Justice of the Community in Chapter V.

[11] See Cmnd. 3301, pp. 8–12.

[12] *Europe: Unification and Law,* Pelican books, Harmondsworth, 1969.

[13] *N.V. Internationale Crediet– en Handels–Vereniging 'Rotterdam'* v. *Minister van Landbouw en Visserij* (case 72/63) *de Cooperatieve Suikerfabriek* and *Raffinaderij G. A. 'Puttershoek'* v. *Minister van Landbouw en Visserij* (case 74/63) before the Court of Justice of the European Communities [1964] C.M.L.R. 199; see also *Costa* v. *ENEL* [1964] C.M.L.R. 425—when there is conflict between Community law and National law, the Treaty prevails and applies directly to member States.

[14] For a discussion of this concept, see Wortley, *Jurisprudence,* Manchester, 1967, pp. 390–400.

[15] McLachlan and Swann, *Competition Policy in the European Community,* London, 1967, at p. 443, observe that 'Competition policy is an important part of general economic policy in any system that is based wholly or to a large extent upon the principles of a market economy. In the Communities it is expected to contribute to exactly the same type of goals as it does in the ordinary national economic framework—lower prices, faster technical progress, and a fairer distribution of income, for example. But in the context of integration competition is also a medium to expedite the unification of the national economies into one larger common market.'

[16] For Council Regulation No. 17 on this see Appendix 3 of the present volume.

[17] In the Common Market White Paper of 1970, Cmnd. 4259, there is envisaged a future Common Market of 300 millions 'from Scotland

to Sicily and from the Irish Republic to the borders of Eastern Europe'.

[18] For partial international economic order, see Schwarzenberger, *Economic World Order?*, Manchester, 1970 (Schill Lecture).

[19] Kos–Rabcewicz–Zubkowski, *East European Rules on the Validity of International Commercial Arbitration Agreements,* Manchester, 1970.

[20] See *The Times,* 4 August 1967; Tao-Tai Hsia and Murray in *Quarterly Journal of the Library of Congress,* October 1968, p. 293.

[21] 'La théorie connaît deux types d'économie, de conduite des diverses activités humaines: l'économie planifiée et l'économie du marché basée sur la concurrence. Ces deux systèmes—on trouve évidemment dans la pratique de nombreuses formes mixtes—sont logiques et cohérents. Ils diffèrent toutefois par une caractéristique essentielle: l'économie planifiée a besoin du commandement de l'autorité étatique, le régime de concurrence fait confiance à la libre décision des agents économiques. Si dans ce dernier cas une juste convergence des activités économiques découle de la multiplicité des décisions, ce phénomène est dû à un système de signalisation, celui des prix de marché, système qui indique è chacun la décision que requiert la réalité économique.'—*Droit des Communautés Européennes—Les Novelles: La Communauté Economique Européenne,* ed. Van der Meersch, Brussels, Section IV, p. 797, para. 1978.

[22] 'L'économie du marché et la concurrence ne constituent sans aucun doute pas des valeurs en soi. Elles sont des formes et des méthodes d'action économique. Elles s'insèrent comme des modèles économiques et sociologiques dans le choix des valeurs sur lesquelles est fondée notre société. En effet, le postulat de la liberté, pierre angulaire de ce choix, confère à la concurrence sa légitimation en tant qu'incarnation du principe de la liberté démocratique en matière économique.'—Van der Meersch, *op. cit.,* p. 798, para. 1979.

[23] See Professor Cohn's *Manual of German Law,* Volumes I and II, London, 1968 and 1971, especially Vol. I, pp. 31 and 32.

[24] For a fuller account, see Wortley, *op. cit.,* Chapters 3, 9 and 10; David, *Major Legal Systems in the World Today,* tr. Brierley, 1968, and *An Introduction to Legal Systems,* ed. Derrett, London, 1968.

[25] Cmnd. 3301, pp. 12 and 13, reprinted as Appendix 1.

[26] Wortley, *op. cit.,* Chapter 11.

Chapter II

THE COMMON MARKET: THE GEOGRAPHICAL AND GENERAL BACKGROUND

Geoffrey North

All students of the Common Market, irrespective of their special field of interest, must recognise a series of key events that eventually led to the signing of the Treaty of Rome on 25 March 1957. Many of these events, such as that of 5 June 1947, when General Marshall proposed United States aid to stimulate the economic recovery of Europe, or that which followed from it on 16 April 1948, when the Organisation for European Economic Co-operation (O.E.E.C.) was created, reflected the character of political, economic and social circumstances that were peculiar to the immediate post-war years; their detailed investigation lies mainly outside the scope and purpose of this chapter. One event does not, however—namely, the proposal of M Robert Schuman on 9 May 1950 to place the utilisation and disposal of French and German coal and steel resources under a common authority. This proposal was remarkable not only in that it was to lead to the setting up of the European Coal and Steel Community (E.C.S.C.) the following year by the six countries that were eventually to establish the European Economic Community, but also because it focused attention for the first time on certain fundamental geographical aspects of an economic situation of long standing.

During the nineteenth century coal had become the dominant source of industrial energy, and the location of manufacturing activity in Western Europe had come to reflect either a direct tie with the coalfield or with points to which coal could be moved cheaply and in bulk. In this latter respect the role of the navigable waterway was of paramount importance: this was clearly demonstrated in the way in which industrial regions had grown up along the river Rhine or in association with the development of the canal networks of north-east France and the Low Countries. Of all industries that displayed such ties, that of iron and steel making was pre-eminent, simply because of the scale of the demand which it made for coal, particularly for the type that could be processed into metallurgical coke for use both as a fuel and as a reducing agent in the blast furnace. Since, however, iron making, at least before the First World War, demanded equally large quantities of iron ore, the most suitable sites other than on the coalfields came to be those at which not only was there coal available, but also where iron ore could be obtained cheaply. In simple terms, three types of suitable location thus emerged in continental Western Europe: on the coalfield, on the orefield and by the waterway, a pattern which has persisted, though with varying emphasis, until the present time. More important still, most major centres were to be found relatively near each other. The Ruhr coalfield, with the richest reserves of coking coal and with a Rhineside location, became the biggest single region of iron and steel manufacturing, and within two hundred miles other important centres grew up, such as those on the Saar coalfield, on and near the orefields of Lorraine, and on the Sambre–Meuse coalfield of Belgium. Moreover, not only were they in such relative proximity to one another but they also grew to be economically interdependent. Although the Ruhr was the major producer of coal, iron and steel, it had to import ore and, in consequence, used the Rhine with Rotterdam as its gateway for the import of overseas ore, and it developed links by rail with the orefields of Lorraine. On the other hand, there was no other centre of iron and steel making, nor indeed any coalfield, that possessed on site such a superabundance of coking coal as the Ruhr; in particular, the French sectors of these industries came to be dependent on it for much of their fuel needs. The Ruhr thus became the biggest single exporter of coal and coke to the rest of continental Western Europe and it was this function, coupled with serving the needs of German iron and steel making, that, in terms of the volume of goods handled, made the Rhine the most important commercial highway in Europe and Duisburg–Ruhrort its biggest inland port.

Juxtaposition and interdependence of industrial raw materials, therefore, were two of the fundamental features associated with the development of heavy industries and energy production in Western Europe. But this interrelationship went much further. As the scale of iron and steel manufacturing expanded and as its products became increasingly specialised, so the complex interdependence of the iron and steel producers for raw materials was paralleled by an equally intricate exchange of iron and steel products that ranged from those which were semi-processed, such as ingots and bars, to those that were finished and of high quality, such as tubes, wire, plate and special constructional steels.[1] Inevitably, trade thus not only moved between the iron and steel producers but, in turn, their products served as the raw materials for other types of manufacturing industry. This movement was at its most intense within that area where heavy industrial interdependence had grown up, for there, above all, was a well-established and efficient network of communications and related industrial services. It was for this reason, for example, that by the inter-war period the Netherlands had come to be Germany's biggest single customer for iron ingots and bars and also for sheet steel.[2] It was no small wonder that the problems which arose from moving such an increasingly wide range of bulky goods and materials across international frontiers—problems that were clearly exacerbated by the effects of war—called for the establishment of some form of international co-ordination and control. Schuman's plan was, to many at least, a logical realisation that if interdependent industries existed in close geographical association, then interchange and production should be made as efficient as possible.

This argument may be extended to explain the reasons that lay behind the proposals for even fuller economic integration made by the Foreign Ministers of the Six when they met at Messina during the first three days of June 1955. It was possible to recognise in geographical terms some degree of interdependence of industry as a whole. Just as the heavy industries of continental Western Europe had developed within a relatively concentrated area, so too had many other principal industries. There were many reasons for this. Coal mining and iron and steel making attracted the development of associated industries such as engineering and chemicals. The availability of good communications offered advantages to all manufacturing industry particularly to develop at those nodal points within the system created by the waterways, the railways and, increasingly this century, the motorways. This process of growth and expansion of industry was accelerated with the increase in the use of electricity as a major source of energy. Grid distribution rendered ties with the coalfields unnecessary for those industries that did not need bulk quantities of coal as a solid fuel. Industry, in consequence, became increasingly market-orientated, and this, at least in locational terms, meant within the growing city regions and along the major transport arteries that joined them. Thus the Rhine valley linked industrial cities from the Swiss Foreland to the North Sea. It was one major axis of vigorous economic growth within the lowlands of north-west Europe that were served by a network of communications at the nodal points of which expanded those cities that had for centuries been centres of industrial production and commercial interchange. Industrial growth in post-war France, for example, continued to be at its most dynamic in and around Paris, where all the advantages of centrality and market orientation were at their greatest. In addition, access to other urban regions in north-west Europe was at its best. Similarly the growth of industry in German cities such as Frankfurt, Stuttgart and Munich, in Brussels in Belgium, and in Milan and Turin in northern Italy, demonstrated the importance of central location, an advantage that has appeared not only abiding but which has seemed to intensify with technological change. Moreover, as affluence in these cities increased, so the range of manufacturing and service trades widened. Thus, just as the iron and steel industries displayed features of interdependence through geographical proximity and the need to exchange surpluses, so too the major urban regions of continental Western Europe grew to be associated within a similar framework.

If one examines a map of Western Europe one cannot fail to note the geographical concentration and juxtaposition not only of the major centres of heavy industry but also of the major urban regions. It is possible to distinguish what has become known to many as the 'core', a region that has within it two major axes. The first extends from Paris north-eastwards across the Low Countries, through the industrial cities of the lower Rhine as far as Hanover; the second runs transversely to it from Rotterdam along the Rhine, intersecting at the Ruhr and continuing to Frankfurt, Strasbourg, Mannheim and the south-western German cities as far as the Swiss border.

Within this core region are all the traditional economic advantages that promote industrial growth: ease of movement, access to raw materials, energy supplies and the products of heavy industry along with the proximity to centres of affluence. In an age of technological change and industrial mergers, where industrial units increase in size to promote greater efficiency, so the need to seek bigger markets intensifies. Motor vehicle manufacturing, for example, with its associations with mass production, city regions and the export trade, has shown itself to be acutely sensitive to these tendencies. A study of this industry in Western Europe would show that the stage has been reached where no major firm can view its market area strictly within a national framework. In France motor vehicle manufacturers, increasingly concentrating their centres of production around Paris, look more towards the affluent urban regions of the Low Countries and Germany as extensions of their markets than towards the country districts of France itself. Similar parallels exist in other consumer goods industries. Thus any proposal to establish within Western Europe an international economic system that permitted industrial production to take place at the point of maximum locational advantage could only confirm a tendency that had been taking place in the industrial geography of the region for at least a century.

But the international economic integration which was envisaged at the Messina Conference in 1955 and subsequently outlined in the Treaty of Rome was not to be confined solely to this affluent and industrially productive core. All regions of the Six and all sectors of their economy were to be involved. It is at this stage that two major problems are to be discerned relating to agriculture and to the economies of those regions peripheral to the core area.

As far as agriculture was concerned, there was neither geographical concentration of production nor international economic interdependence on anything like the scale of industry. Before the creation of the E.E.C. the situation was quite the reverse. It was inevitable, of course, that agricultural activity exhibited widespread regional variation, in so far as it was conditioned by a wide range of environmental factors where the opportunities and restrictions presented by climate, soils and water supplies played no small part. In these respects variations in natural endowment existed between each country. France was the most favoured: it was the largest country in the E.E.C. and possessed land suitable for agricultural use which was greater in area than that of Germany and Italy put together. There were parts of the Paris basin, for example, where the natural advantages for the production of cereal foodstuffs, notably wheat, were the finest in Europe. Germany, in contrast, suffered a greater degree of natural drawbacks, with its colder winters, with poor soils covering many of those parts of its lowlands that had suffered glaciation, and in the highland areas of the southern half of the country, where difficult terrain and acid soils were all too abundant. In Italy natural conditions in many regions were even worse: along so much of the rugged Appennine spine of the country summer droughts, limestone tracts and thin soils had long brought problems associated with the provision of surface water supplies. These problems were particularly bad in the southern half of the country, known as the Mezzogiorno. Even France had its problem areas in the isolated mountainous parts of the Massif Central, the Alps and Brittany.

Regional variations in the prosperity of agriculture were further affected by systems of ownership and farming methods. Land holdings in many parts of France, Italy and, above all, Germany were dominated by the strip system of farming, where each farm comprised a set of geographically separated fields and plots. Their scattered nature owed much to the effects of inheritance laws that had, through equal division to heirs over many decades, produced a bewildering mosaic of parcels of land. In Germany, in particular, this fragmentation was at its worst in the naturally least favoured areas: in the Jura of northern Bavaria and in the Rhine uplands of Hesse and the Palatinate. Larger farms had their problems as well, especially in southern Italy, where much estate farming in difficult terrain had been associated with socially restrictive practices and under-use of labour, all of which was aggravated by the problems of over-population.

The crux of the agrarian problem, however, lay in protectionism. Whereas industrial growth in so many parts of continental Western Europe had promoted closer international ties, there was little parallel in agriculture. All countries levied tariffs on imported foodstuffs, a policy which had been adopted to protect domestic agriculture from suffering the effects of competition from cheaper foodstuffs imported from the New World. To countries like Italy and France this policy had long remained essential, as they had been slow to industrialise and could not offer employment opportunities on a scale similar to that which obtained in Britain and Germany. Even as late as 1958, France had nearly 25 per cent of its employed population in agriculture, and Italy had over 30 per cent. Protectionism had, however, brought its own problems, as it had so often permitted the inefficient farmer to survive on land that was too poor to sustain high crop yields, on farms that were fragmented and were, above all, too small. At the time of the signing of the Rome Treaty over two-thirds of all the farms in the Federal Republic of Germany were less than ten hectares (approximately twenty-five acres) in size, and in France the proportion was 60 per cent, with marked concentrations of small farms in the western and south-western parts of the country—in those parts where the range of employment opportunity was at its most restricted. The advent of the Common Market, therefore, designed as it was to bring about the progressive reduction of tariffs on foodstuffs moving across national frontiers within the E.E.C., suddenly exposed international differences not only in natural endowment but also in the type, structure and efficiency of farming.

Such variety was most marked in the prices for produce paid to farmers. The highest prices for wheat, barley and beef cattle were paid in Germany, a reflection of the harsher terrain and climate and the inefficient state of farming in those parts where there was extreme sub-division of land holdings. France, on the other hand, paid the lowest prices for these foodstuffs, and the Netherlands and Belgium paid the lowest for dairy produce. Yields, too, varied from country to country. Though France was a low-cost producer, it had the second lowest yields for grains and meat, only Italy being lower. In Germany and the Netherlands yields for these products were the highest among the Six, for they reflected the attempts made by farmers, within a protected system, and in a difficult terrain, to provide foodstuffs for urban communities in the growing industrial regions.

Potentially, France had the best agricultural prospects within an economically integrated Europe. By making its farming more efficient, and thus more productive, the resulting surpluses could be absorbed within the extended market area provided that price levels were maintained to its advantage and levies were imposed on foodstuffs imported from outside the E.E.C. And this is precisely what happened. Germany, so much the industrial 'kingpin' of the Common Market, was complemented by France, with its rich farmlands. Walter Lippmann's interesting assertion that the Common Market was 'a bargain between French agriculture and German industry'[3] seemed to hold true, at least in 1958 when the Treaty of Rome came into force.

This treaty was, however, designed to promote economic integration on a much wider scale than this and it had to take note of the serious regional imbalances that existed in economic prosperity. The 'core' area of the Common Market seemed to possess all the advantages, for not only were the major concentrations of industry and commercial exchange here, but in the Paris basin and the lowlands of the lower Rhine farming was at its most productive and efficient. In complete contrast, there were regions peripheral to this centre where distance from markets, difficult terrain and lack of economic resources had long prevented the development of a wide and attractive range of employment opportunities. In these areas the population was over-dependent on an agricultural system that was in itself as deprived of natural advantages as it was inefficient in method. Central Brittany was such an area. In 1960 the income per head of the population was only half that of the Paris region. In Corsica it was less than a quarter.[4] In both problem areas the opportunities to increase wealth were restricted by the poverty of natural resources and isolation from the major economic growth points in France. Broadly speaking, much of western and highland France suffered in this way. In Italy there were similar, if not worse, problems. Contrasts existed between the prosperity of the north and the Mezzogiorno that were not only of long standing but which had increased during the present century as industry had developed in the northern cities, and destitution and unemployment had grown in the south.[5]

Such regional imbalances were not merely a function of distance from the centre and poverty of natural resources. There were, in addition, regions of industrial depression and slow economic growth associated with some coalfield areas within the core region of the E.E.C. Along the Sambre–Meuse valley in Belgium coal mining, one of the region's staple industries, was facing in the post-war period severe economic problems with the exhaustion of the better types of coal and the increased cost of working in seriously faulted seams. Added to this, the economic incentives to introduce replacement industries weakened as industrial opportunities were increasingly focused on the plain of Flanders and within the Brussels conurbation. It was a problem that was not dissimilar to that facing many British coalfields in their schemes for industrial redevelopment.

Finally, there were those regions where economic difficulties had arisen as a result of changing political circumstances. Nowhere was this more true than in Germany in those districts bordering the Iron Curtain. Population decline had begun to take place by the end of the 1950's, and business confidence and investment opportunity remained weak as political and economic separation from the eastern half of Germany persisted. Even Hamburg, for all its rebuilding and apparent economic recovery, felt the effects of this division, which had cut off over half its traditional hinterland. Considerable adjustments had to be made in its commercial function and it grew to handle specialised cargo for the markets of north-west Germany. Even so, such re-orientation brought other problems as Hamburg was compelled to compete with ports such as Rotterdam which enjoyed a more central location.

Problem regions within the E.E.C. were not solely confined, therefore, to areas that had suffered long-standing economic disadvantage. The varied character of such regions presented a serious challenge to those concerned with the formulation of a common regional policy, and it is not surprising to find that to date no such policy has been effective in redressing regional imbalances.

Since the Common Market came into effect, principally since 1959, when the first tariff reductions were made, several changes in the economic geography of the six member countries have taken place. In many ways they represent an intensification of processes that had been long under way; in other cases, new distributional patterns have emerged.

There has been a tremendous growth both in the scale and in the nature of industrial activity within the E.E.C. Predictably, this growth has been most marked within the central core area. In France, Paris has continued to dominate urban and industrial life. Any conscious attempt on the part of government to decentralise industry by placing development restrictions within Paris itself has pushed relocation but a short distance from the conurbation, particularly down the Seine and towards the north.[6] In Belgium, similar industrial attractions have persisted in Antwerp and Brussels, whilst in the Netherlands severe planning restrictions have had to be placed on the nature and direction of industrial and urban sprawl in the *Randstad*, the central arc of cities that extends from Rotterdam, through The Hague and Amsterdam to Hilversum and Utrecht. In Germany, notwithstanding the decline of coal mining within the inner zone of the Rhine–Ruhr industrial region, the conurbation as a whole has continued to grow. Its prosperity demonstrates the abiding advantage of centrality within an international communications system.

Throughout the 1960's the increasing use of electricity accentuated industrial ties with the market centres. The most recent developments in the supply and use of other sources of energy, notably oil and natural gas, seem only to have intensified this pattern. Oil is received in colossal quantities by ports that must be constantly re-equipped to handle bigger tankers. If these ports do not lie within the core region then the oil and its products are piped to it. A network of pipelines extends from the Mediterranean ports of Marseilles, Genoa and Trieste as far as the middle Rhine valley and central Bavaria, where refineries at Strasbourg, Karlsruhe and Ingolstadt serve the industrial centres of eastern France and southern Germany. In northern France oil from Le Havre is piped to Grandpuits, within easy access of Paris. The attraction of the core region is pre-eminent in the spectacular growth of the port of Rotterdam, where Dutch engineering skill and commercial expertise have been quick to exploit the considerable locational advantage that this port has enjoyed for just over a century. In the late 1930's it handled an average of 35 million tons of goods each year. By 1960, with the enlargement of the port westwards to the North Sea to create Europoort, it handled 80 million tons, and by 1970 the total volume of goods handled exceeded the staggering total of 180 million tons.[7] In these terms it is by far the greatest port in the world. Oil imports of nearly 100 million tons dominate its trade and much of its economic life. Oil is refined at the port and has thereby generated industrial activity on a scale undreamed of before the war, though it has brought with it serious problems of atmospheric pollution which demand constant planning control. In addition, pipelines and river barges transport oil and its products to inland industrial sites within the Netherlands and, above all, to the Rhine–Ruhr conurbation, thus strengthening traditional ties of economic interdependence.

It is only a matter of academic interest to assess in precise terms the beneficial effects that customs union has had on economic growth within such regions.[8] This growth has remained centralised on major transport axes and its geographical manifestations have brought few surprises.

It is perhaps outside the urban and industrial core region that Common Market policy has had the most marked geographical consequences. Nowhere is this more true than in the agricultural areas. Whereas the implementation of tariff reductions and quota enlargement policies simply accelerated industrial growth along well-established lines, the Common Market Agricultural Policy has sought to establish some degree and pattern of integration which, as we have seen, never previously existed. The C.A.P. has continued to protect the agriculture of the member countries as a whole from the possible dangers of outside competition, through the establishment of a unified system of variable import levies. At the same time it has attempted to establish within the E.E.C. a system of price guarantees to all farmers. This has had the unfortunate effect of encouraging farmers to produce far more foodstuffs than could be absorbed in the home market. When harvests were good, huge surpluses accumulated and they were taken into stock or disposed of through a system of export subsidies. So costly did this mechanism prove that little collective attention could be paid by the E.E.C. to improve the structure of farming and, in particular, its efficiency. Protection and price support continued to permit all but the poorest endowed farmer to survive. Fundamentally, therefore, the Common Market faced exactly the same problems in 1968 as it had in 1958, except that in some areas they had worsened. In France agricultural output rose by 40 per cent during these ten years, the most remarkable increases being recorded for wheat, the average annual output of which had risen from 9 million tons to 15 million tons.[9] Except for the remoter parts of western Brittany, the central Pyrenees and parts of the Massif Central, no areas recorded decreases in production. Substantial increases in areas under cultivation of wheat took place within the most favoured parts of the Paris basin. This situation was paralleled in other parts of the Common Market, where even in Germany increases in output were recorded over extensive areas as well as increases in areas under cultivation in Schleswig-Holstein and lower Saxony. The C.A.P. thus seemed to favour all regions, irrespective of their natural resources and farming systems. Massive increases occurred in the production of maize, particularly in France, and—most notorious of all—in the production of butter, where dairy farming, encouraged by price guarantees, spread to areas that had never previously developed it for commercial purposes. And yet so much farming remained in the hands of the smallholder: in 1969 over 60 per cent of all farms in the E.E.C. were less than 10 hectares in size, and over 80 per cent of all dairy farms had herds of fewer than twenty-five cows. Worst of all, too many farmers have remained on the land, for in 1969 they numbered 10 million and constituted over 15 per cent of the total labour force of the E.E.C., despite the great increases that had taken place in the range of employment opportunities. Through the initiative of Sicco Mansholt, the C.A.P. has undergone a revision that has been formally accepted by the Agricultural Ministers of the Six after a three-day session in March 1971. The emphasis has been switched from price support to the structural reform of farming. Such reform involves the reorganisation of farms into larger units, the introduction of mechanical methods, and the redeployment of labour as well as the pensioning off of farmers at the age of 55. Though each country has attempted to introduce reforms along these lines for some years, it is the first time that a co-ordinated and adequately financed policy has been attempted, and it is too early to comment on the likely geographical effects of these changes.

But no matter what reforms and policy changes are introduced in whatever sector or region of the E.E.C., it is difficult to escape from the fact that regional disparities in economic and social opportunity persist. Though the population of the Community continues to grow and now exceeds 190 million nothing of any fundamental importance has changed in the principal pattern of its distribution. Population concentration, coupled with whatever opportunities the geographical accidents of location and resource endowment may bring, will long remain features that no student of the E.E.C. can ever afford to ignore.

NOTES

[1] For a fuller discussion of this theme see British Iron and Steel Federation, 'The interdependence of the European coal and steel industries', *Monthly Statistical Bulletin,* Vol. 25, No. 5, May 1950.

[2] League of Nations, *International Trade Statistics, 1938,* Geneva, 1939, pp. 27 and 229–231.

[3] Lippmann, *Western Unity and the Common Market,* London, 1962, p. 14.

[4] Barzanti, *The Underdeveloped Areas within the Common Market,* Princeton, N.J., 1967, pp. 89–90.

[5] Montini, 'The Parliamentary enquiry into destitution in Italy' (summary report), *International Labour Review,* Vol. 31, No. 1, January 1955, p. 8.

[6] Clout, 'Industrial relocation in France', *Geography,* Vol. 55, Part 1, No. 246, January 1970, pp. 48–63.

[7] These statistics have been obtained from the annual statistical reviews published by the Port of Rotterdam (*Stichting Havenbelangen: Haven van Rotterdam: Statistisch Overzicht*).

[8] *Economic Integration in Europe,* ed. Denton, Chapter 1; Nils Lundgren, *Customs Unions of Industrialised West European Countries,* London, 1969, pp. 25–54.

[9] These statistics and all others relating to agriculture that follow have been taken from the *Yearbook of Agricultural Statistics* (*Agrarstatistisches Jahrbuch: Statistisches Amt der Europäischen Gemeinschaften*), Brussels, 1970.

Chapter III

PREPARING THE AUTHENTIC ENGLISH TEXT OF THE E.E.C. TREATY

Michael Akehurst

Even before the Treaty establishing the European Economic Community entered into force, the Secretariat of the Interim Committee for the Common Market and Euratom requested members of the translation departments of the European Coal and Steel Community and of the Council of Europe to translate the Treaty into English; this translation was published by the Secretariat and has also been printed in volume 298 of the United Nations Treaty Series and in Campbell and Thompson's *Common Market Law: Texts and Commentaries* (London, 1962).

The Foreign Office made its own translation, which was published by H.M. Stationery Office in 1962. A revised translation was produced by the Foreign Office in 1963 and used for internal purposes, but never put on sale to the public. A further revised Foreign Office translation was published in 1967.

Each of these successive translations represents, on balance, an improvement on its predecessor. I say 'on balance' because each of them, while correcting some of the mistakes which appeared in its predecessor, also introduced new mistakes which had not appeared in its predecessor, so that each translation, so to speak, took four steps forward and three steps back.[1]

During the summer of 1970 I worked in the English Translation Section of the Commission of the European Communities, revising the translation of the E.E.C. Treaty. I also revised the translations of the Convention on Certain Institutions Common to the European Communities, of the Treaty establishing a Single Council and a Single Commission of the European Communities (the Merger Treaty), of Regulation 17 on restrictive practices, and of a large number of provisions concerning the Court of Justice of the European Communities.

Early in 1971 the English Translation Section of the Commission recruited other English lawyers to carry on with the same type of work, this time concentrating upon revising the Foreign Office translations of the regulations, directives and decisions issued under the E.E.C. Treaty;[2] I went back to Brussels for a month during the Easter vacation to help with this work. The Foreign Office hopes that the revision of the translations will be completed by 31 December 1971. In fact, despite the help of computers, no one has yet been able to count the number of regulations, etc., which would be applicable to the United Kingdom if it joined the E.E.C.; but the figure usually bandied about in Brussels is 3,500.[3] This figure may turn out to be an exaggeration, but, even so, it will be realised that the Foreign Office's hope of finishing the process of revision by 31 December 1971 is rather optimistic. One reason why the process will take much longer is that the original Foreign Office translations of the various regulations, etc., are very uneven, and sometimes much worse than the Foreign Office translations of the Treaty; in one regulation, for instance, the Foreign Office actually translated *quatre-vingt-cinq* as 'twenty-five'! Mistakes of this sort are easy to correct, but mistranslations of technical legal and economic terms require a good deal of research before they can be corrected.

The object of the exercise is to produce English texts which will be equally authentic with the four original texts. Obviously a task of such importance cannot be carried out by individual translators; the authentic English text has to be agreed by the Community and the United Kingdom government (and also the government of the Irish Republic). During the winter of 1970–71 a joint Working Party on the Authentic English Texts (A.E.T.) was set up. The Commission is represented on the working party by Mr Bastiaan van der Esch, a Dutch member of the Commission's Legal Service (who is also chairman of the working party), assisted by Mr George MacGregor, the Head of the Commission's English Translation Section, and by other members of the Commission's English Translation Section and Legal Service. The United Kingdom is represented by Mr Alexander Elkin, the Special Legal Adviser on European Communities Law in the Foreign and Commonwealth Office, assisted by Mr Mark Marshall, an economist and member of the United Kingdom delegation to the European Communities, and by members of the Translation Section of the European Integration Department of the Foreign and Commonwealth Office. Representatives of the Irish Republic also sit on the working party. It should not be thought, however, that there are opposing 'sides' on the working party. The problems with which it deals are essentially technical ones, which are settled in a spirit of co-operation, not confrontation.

The working party has now provisionally agreed the English text of the E.E.C. Treaty, and, when I was last in Brussels in April 1971, was working on the Treaty establishing the European Coal and Steel Community and on regulations and directives made under the E.E.C. Treaty.

A steering group, composed of other representatives of the Commission and of the United Kingdom, is dealing with the separate problem of the technical amendments which will have to be made to these various instruments in order to adapt them to the needs of an enlarged Community in general, and to the special circumstances of the United Kingdom in particular. (I say 'technical amendments' because the Six have made it very clear, and the United Kingdom has agreed, that amendments on matters of important policy must be kept to a minimum; in any case, amendments on matters of important policy would have to be dealt with at a much higher level.)

The treaties establishing the E.E.C. and Euratom, and all the regulations and most of the directives and decisions issued thereunder, are in four languages, each of which is equally authentic[4]—French, German, Italian and Dutch. (The French text, however, is the only authentic text of the Treaty establishing the E.C.S.C.) Obviously, the English version must try to reflect all four of the original texts, and not merely one of them; and this is no easy task when the four original texts diverge from one another. I am not suggesting that such divergences appear in every article of the E.E.C. Treaty; nevertheless, they do sometimes occur, and they make life very difficult for the translator.[5]

At least as far as the E.E.C. Treaty is concerned, most of the divergences are between the French and German texts. By comparison, the Italian text rarely diverges from the French. The Dutch text sometimes follows the German text and sometimes follows the French one; at other times it uses long paraphrases to express ideas which are conveyed by a few words in the other languages. These paraphrases can be helpful when they explain complicated ideas in simple words (e.g. the paraphrase explaining the meaning of 'droit syndical' in Article 118); but they can also be inaccurate. On the whole, the Dutch text is the least reliable of the four.

There have been many cases in which the Court of Justice of the European Communities has compared the four texts, but there has, so far as I know, been no case where the main point at issue was a discrepancy among the different texts of the Treaty. However, such a case has arisen in connection with a decision issued under the Treaty; but, since I have discussed this case elsewhere, I shall say no more about it today.[6]

When I was working on the E.E.C. Treaty in 1970, I took the 1967 Foreign Office translation as my starting point, because it was the most recent and, on balance, the best translation available at that time (although I did look at others as well); also, I thought that it would be bad politics (and untrue) to tell the Foreign Office, in effect, that their latest translation was not even worth considering and that we ought to start again from scratch. The Foreign Office translators seem to have relied mainly, if not entirely, on the French text of the E.E.C. Treaty. Although I looked at the other languages as well, I too tended to rely on the French text of the Treaty more than on the other three, simply because I knew French better than the other languages; I have a rough knowledge of Italian, but very little of German and Dutch, which meant that, when examining the German and Dutch texts, I had to rely on dictionaries and on discussions with my colleagues. You may think that work of this sort should not have been given to somebody who did not have a good command of all four languages; but at that time there was simply no one available who fulfilled the optimum requirements—English mother tongue, good knowledge of all four languages, and good knowledge of the legal and other points dealt with in the Treaty. In any case, it was surprising how soon I got used to working in five languages at once (i.e. the four original languages, plus English).

In addition to examining the four original texts and various translations of the Treaty, when I was dealing with particularly difficult points I used to consult experts in various departments of the Commission and various commentaries which had been published on the Treaty (some of these were particularly useful, since they contained such *travaux préparatoires* as had been published in respect of the E.E.C. Treaty). I also had access to a number of files which contained records of discussions that had taken place earlier within the Commission on the subject of English translations of the E.E.C. Treaty. Perhaps I ought to say a word about these files. Most of them dated from 1962, i.e. from the period of the first British application to join the E.E.C. Each of the Commission's departments had at that time been asked to comment on the Foreign Office translation of those provisions of the E.E.C Treaty which were of particular concern to it; the English text of a few articles of the Treaty had actually been agreed between the United Kingdom government and the Commission when the negotiations for British entry were suspended early in 1963. The Foreign Office also consulted the Commission on isolated points in 1966, when it was preparing the translation which was published in 1967; and I had access to the records of these consultations too.

Now I would like to say something about how I dealt with discrepancies among the four original texts of the Treaty. I cannot claim to have worked out any clear rules in advance before tackling this problem; however, as time went on, I developed various rough-and-ready rules, which I would like to describe to you.

I was sometimes tempted to give preference to the language in which a provision had been drafted, over the other three languages. There is some authority in favour of this approach to be found in judicial and arbitral decisions dealing with the interpretation of other treaties.[7] Now, it is known that French and German were the drafting languages during the negotiations which produced the E.E.C. Treaty,[8] but it is not always known which articles were drafted in which language; some articles were originally drafted in French, and amendments made in German, or vice versa. Of course, if the French and German texts meant one thing, and the Dutch and Italian texts meant another, I would follow the French and German texts, but I cannot remember this happening; in most cases, where the four texts were not unanimous, the French and German texts were usually found on opposite sides, so to speak. In any case, all four texts are supposed to be equally authentic, so one cannot disregard the Dutch and Italian texts entirely; at the most, one can only give a certain preference to the French and German texts over the Dutch and Italian ones.

Another tempting solution would be to apply a rule of numbers —if three texts mean one thing and the fourth means another, the English text should follow the majority view. But this solution is too mechanical to be applied invariably. What happens, for instance, if the outnumbered text is in the drafting language? Besides, this sort of solution is no use when the discrepancy does not take the form of 'three against one'—for instance, if it takes the form of 'two against two', or if each of the four texts means a different thing!

On the whole, I prefer less mechanical criteria. For instance, if some texts are clear and others are ambiguous, I would prefer to follow the clear texts, provided that the ambiguous texts are capable of being reconciled with the clear texts; in this way one attains a harmony (albeit a rather shaky harmony) between all four texts, which one would not attain by adopting another possible meaning of the ambiguous texts which was not supported by the clear texts.[9] We got so used to this technique in the English Translation Section that my colleagues who were working on the E.C.S.C. Treaty used to resolve ambiguities in the authentic French text by looking at the non-authentic German text.

Again, I sought to reconcile apparently divergent texts by trying to understand the function or purpose of the rule involved. This teleological approach is particularly desirable where the four versions are not precise translations of each other but each is 'angled' according to the economic structure of the member State or States concerned.

In addition, I used to try, where possible, to follow the text which harmonised best with other provisions of the Treaty or with the spirit of the Treaty as a whole—or which was compatible[10] with subsequent developments in the law, in the form of judicial decisions, academic commentaries, administrative practice, and rules enacted to implement the provision in question. For instance, the 1967 translation of Article 85 of the E.E.C. Treaty talks of restrictive practices which may 'affect' trade between member States; a better literal translation of the original texts would be 'impair', but I left 'affect' unaltered because it was more in keeping with the case law of the Court of Justice of the European Communities.

This brings me on to another point—to what extent can one disregard the literal meaning of the original texts (even when there is no discrepancy among them) if it appears that the literal meaning does not reflect what the drafters intended to say, or the way in which a provision is applied in practice? Well, at times I did 'stretch' the literal meaning of the texts, as in Article 85; but on the whole I took the line that my job was to translate the Treaty, not to improve it. For instance, the first paragraph of Article 174 of the E.E.C. Treaty provides: 'Si le recours est fondé, la Cour de Justice déclare nul et non avenu l'acte contesté.' These words—and the corresponding words in the other three languages—imply that the Court's judgment is merely declaratory of a pre-existing nullity. The Court's case law, however, makes it crystal-clear that what the Court does in a *recours en annulation* is to annul an act which was valid until annulled; the act is voidable, not void. But a translator's job is to translate what is actually said, not to translate what he thinks ought to have been said. Similarly, if all the original texts are ambiguous, this ambiguity has got to remain in the English version.

Technical legal terms are often difficult to translate, because the law varies from country to country. Some of the legal terms used in Community law, although borrowed from Continental systems of law, can be translated surprisingly well into English; for others, there is no exact counterpart. In such cases the best thing to do is to use non-technical terms in English, or even to create new terms, and hope that English lawyers will gradually come to attribute a technical meaning to these terms as they become more familiar with community law (e.g. 'misuse of power' as a translation of *détournement de pouvoir*). The fatal mistake is to use technical terms of English law which sound like a French term but which do not mean the same thing. For instance, Article 26 of the Merger Treaty talks of various types of wrongful act committed by a Community employee 'dans l'exercice de ses fonctions'; this *sounds* like the good old English 'course of employment', and was so translated by the Foreign Office, but the judgment of the Court of Justice of the European Communities in *Sayag* v. *Leduc*[11] makes it clear that the French words have a very much more limited meaning, and I therefore suggested that the English version be altered. Another reason for not using technical terms of English law is that the Treaty has to be intelligible in Scotland as well as in England, and Scots law is so different from English law that a technical term of English law might have an entirely different meaning, or no meaning at all, in Scotland. Finally, it must be remembered that the Treaty is quadrilingual, and an over-precise translation of a French legal term like *détournement de pouvoir* might very well not do justice to the terms used in the other three languages, which do not mean precisely the same thing; so a less technical translation is preferable.

If the United Kingdom joins the E.E.C., it seems to be generally accepted that English will become an official language of the Communities, and that the English text of the Treaties and of the various regulations, etc., issued under the Treaties will become equally authentic with the original texts. But if the United Kingdom joins the E.E.C., the Republic of Ireland, Denmark and Norway will also join the E.E.C. in all probability; and what will happen as regards *their* languages? I think it unlikely that Irish will become an official language of the Communities; the Republic of Ireland tried at one time to enact authentic Irish texts as well as English texts of all its statutes, but soon abandoned the attempt, and nowadays only a few of the statutes passed by the Oireachtas have an authentic Irish text as well as an English text. (It is true that the Irish government often translates statutes into Irish, but the translations are usually made for purposes of information only, and seldom have the status of authentic texts.) Danish and Norwegian represent more of a problem. It would be difficult for the Communities to operate with seven official languages; it would cost a lot of time and money to draft everything in seven languages, and the possibility of discrepancies among the different texts increases in proportion to the number of the texts. But a large amount of Community law is applicable in municipal courts, and a dualist approach, in which Denmark, say, would apply texts in Danish as part of Danish law, while being bound on the international plane by texts in other languages, would open up the possibility of a disturbing divergence between Community law and municipal law; if Danish courts applied a Danish text which did not faithfully reflect the authentic texts, Denmark might find herself being sued in the Court of Justice of the European Communities for failing to fulfil her obligations under Community law. If Danish and Norwegian are not going to become official languages of the Communities, the only solution appears to be that Danish and Norwegian courts, when applying rules of Community law, should apply the authentic texts, which would be in languages other than Danish and Norwegian. This may seem to place a heavy strain on the linguistic abilities of Danish and Norwegian lawyers and judges, but I believe that one Scandinavian country has already enacted the English text of a treaty as part of its municipal law; so there are precedents for this process.

If the English text becomes equally authentic with the original text, this means that the Six will become bound by the English text as well as by the original texts. No translation is perfect, and there are bound to be a few discrepancies between the English text and the original texts; the result, in effect, will be a slight amendment to the Treaty. But it must be remembered that the entry of the United Kingdom into the Communities will automatically change Community law, even if English texts do *not* become equally authentic. The reason is that gaps in Community law are filled by recourse to the general principles of law common to the member States, and the entry of a new member State whose law differs from the laws of the existing member States will automatically produce changes in this area of Community law, if in no others.[12]

In conclusion, I want to say something about the way in which English courts ought to interpret the E.E.C. Treaty if the United Kingdom joins the Communities. When interpreting statutes, English courts generally apply strict rules of interpretation; in particular, they presume that a difference of terminology implies a difference of meaning. The Foreign Office translations of the E.E.C. Treaty frequently used different English words in different articles to translate the same French words. The Working Party on Authentic English Texts is paying particular attention to eradicating this type of inconsistency, but it would be optimistic to expect them to succeed in every single case. Besides, Continental lawyers (and international lawyers) adopt a much looser style of drafting than English lawyers, and very often the original texts of the Treaty use different words in different places to express the same idea. It is inevitable that an English translation will reflect the same style of draftsmanship; and the application of strict English rules of statutory interpretation to such a text would produce absurd results.

There are similar problems of interpretation which may also arise. If the English text inadvertently uses an expression which has a technical meaning in English law, must an English court interpret it in accordance with that technical meaning? Can an English court look at foreign language texts? Can it look at *travaux préparatoires*?

All these questions are really part of a wider problem—should English courts apply English law rules of interpretation or international law rules of interpretation?[13]

This problem has arisen before in connection with other treaties. According to an article by I. M. Sinclair, of the Foreign Office,[14] the answer normally depends on the procedure used to give effect to the Treaty in English law. If the Act of Parliament giving effect to the Treaty in English law does not use the exact words of the

Treaty, then the ordinary English law rules of interpretation apply. If the Act of Parliament incorporates the actual text (or part of the text) of the Treaty, then there is a possibility that English courts will apply international law rules of interpretation; however, the cases conflict, although the cases decided since Sinclair wrote have reinforced the tendency to apply international law rules of interpretation,[15] even when the statute in question does not incorporate the actual words of the Treaty.[16] All the same, to be on the safe side, it might perhaps be desirable to insert a section in the relevant Act of Parliament directing the courts to construe it in accordance with international law rules of interpretation.[17] Such a section would not be unlike the clause used in the Uniform Laws of the United States: 'Uniformity of interpretation: This Act shall be so interpreted and construed as to effectuate its general purpose to make uniform the laws of those States who enact it.'

NOTES

[1] For comparison between the 1962 and 1967 Foreign Office translations, see Maas, 'The English version of the Treaty of Rome', 6 *C.M.L. Rev.* (1969), 205, at pp. 206–8.

[2] Article 189 of the E.E.C. Treaty provides:

'Pour l'accomplissement de leur mission et dans les conditions prévues au présent Traité, le Conseil et la Commission arrêtent des règlements et des directives, prennent des décisions et formulent des recommandations ou des avis.

'Le règlement a une portée générale. Il est obligatoire dans tous ses éléments et il est directement applicable dans tout État membre.

'La directive lie tout État membre destinataire quant au résultat à atteindre, tout en laissant aux instances nationales la compétence quant à la forme et aux moyens.

'La décision est obligatoire en tous ses éléments pour les destinataires qu'elle désigne.

'Les recommandations et les avis ne lient pas.'

[3] In case the sheer volume of these rules should be used as an argument against the United Kingdom joining the E.E.C., it is sobering to recall that the United Kingdom normally issues about 2,000 statutory instruments each year. A number of the E.E.C. regulations, etc., will simply *replace* rules which are at present contained in United Kingdom statutes and statutory instruments, so that the entry of the United Kingdom into the E.E.C. will not greatly increase the *volume* of law to be applied by United Kingdom courts, although it will of course change the source and substance of part of that law.

[4] Article 248 of the E.E.C. Treaty provides: 'This Treaty, drawn up in a single original in the French, German, Italian and Netherlands

languages, all four texts being equally authentic, shall be deposited in the archives of the Government of the Italian Republic, which shall transmit a certified copy to each of the Governments of the other signatory States.'

[5] On the other hand, a translator who despairs of the possibility of completely eliminating discrepancies between the English text and the original texts can derive consolation from the existence of discrepancies among the four original texts; if the Community has survived despite discrepancies among the four original texts, it will surely be able to survive despite discrepancies between the authentic English text and the original texts.

[6] *Stauder* v. *City of Ulm (Sozialamt), Recueil de la jurisprudence,* Vol. 15, 1969, and case-note in 44 *B.Y.I.L.* (1970) 242.

[7] Hardy, 'The interpretation of plurilingual texts by international courts and tribunals', 37 *B.Y.I.L.* (1961) 72, at pp. 98–106. See also the *Stauder* case, referred to in note 6.

[8] When the Treaty was signed on Monday 25 March 1957 only a rough draft existed of the Dutch and Italian texts; as far as these texts were concerned, the Treaty was signed 'in blank', and the texts added later (*pace* Article 248 of the Treaty, which says that it was 'drawn up in a single original in the German, French, Italian and Dutch languages'). The work of bringing the French and German texts into line with one another continued until dawn on Sunday 24 March; even so, a number of discrepancies had to be removed after the Treaty was signed (and others were never noticed or removed). See Maas, *loc. cit.*, p. 205.

[9] There is judicial and arbitral authority in favour of this process of interpretation: Hardy, *loc. cit.*, pp. 82–91.

[10] I use the word 'compatible' deliberately; a translation which fitted subsequent developments in the law *too* closely would be bad, because it would leave no room for the law to develop in a different direction in the future. The Court of Justice of the European Communities, for instance, is not bound by its previous decisions, although it usually follows them.

[11] *Recueil de la jurisprudence,* Vol. 15, 1969, p. 329, and case-note in 44 *B.Y.I.L.* (1970) 240.

[12] For instance, the rules of English law concerning the withdrawal of administrative decisions are completely different from Continental rules on this subject: compare the *Algera case, Recueil de la jurisprudence,* Vol. 3, 1957, pp. 81, 115, with Ganz, 'Estoppel and *res judicata* in administrative law', *Public Law,* 1965, p. 237. But this is an isolated example; even in administrative law the difference between Continental systems and English law is mainly a matter of details, not of principles. For instance, in disputes between the Communities and their staff the Court of Justice of the European Communities has applied general principles of administrative law which exist in common law countries as well as on the Continent; it is no coincidence that the same principles have been applied by the Administrative Tribunals of the United Nations and of the International Labour Organisation, which include Judges from common law countries. See Akehurst, *The Law governing*

Employment in International Organizations, London, 1967, chapters 7 and 12–15.

[13] This problem is only partly solved by the possibility of referring cases to the Court of Justice of the European Communities under Article 177 of the E.E.C. Treaty. Why should litigants be put to the extra expense and trouble of arguing a case in Luxembourg on a simple point of interpretation which an English court ought to be able to solve on its own? Besides, a court which is insular about questions of interpretation is likely to be even more insular about referring cases to the Court of the Communities.

[14] 'The principles of treaty interpretation and their application by the English Courts', 12 *I.C.L.Q.* (1963) 508.

[15] *Corocraft Ltd* v. *Pan American Airways Inc.* [1969] 1 Q.B. 616.

[16] *Post Office* v. *Estuary Radio Ltd.* [1967] 1 W.L.R. 847, 864–5. See also *Salomon* v. *Commissioners of Customs and Excise* [1967] 2 Q.B. 116.

[17] This presupposes that the rules of interpretation are the same in Community law and in international law. So they are, on the whole, although it is possible that there may be one or two exceptions; see 44 *B.Y.I.L.* (1970) 244, note 2.

Note. After this book went to press the negotiators in Brussels agreed that there shall be an authentic text of the E.E.C. Treaty in Irish, and authentic texts in English, Danish and Norwegian of the E.E.C. Treaty and of the regulations and directives issued under the Treaty (cf. p. 26 above).

For an example of the French text of a treaty being enacted as part of Italian law, see *Re Masini,* 24 *I.L.R.* (1957) 11.

Chapter IV

COMPANY LAW AND THE COMMON MARKET: THE FIRST STEP

J. A. Emlyn Davies

The subject I have been permitted to choose is one with which I have been concerned in the course of my official duties and I am sure that it will readily be understood that I cannot properly discuss questions of government policy or the course of our negotiations with the institutions of the Community. What I shall try to set out is the result of a lengthy process of trying to see (*a*) how the requirements of a particular part of Community law would affect English law and (*b*) how those requirements would need to be adapted in order that they should have the same effect on our laws as they have or are intended to have on the laws of the existing members of the Community. Hence this chapter is not so much an attempt to convey information as an essay in appreciation based on a close study, for strictly practical purposes, of a particular part of the fabric of Community law.

So far the only provision of Community law which involves changes in the company law of the member States is the directive of the Council of 9 March 1968, or, to give it its full and rather formidable title:

THE FIRST DIRECTIVE OF THE COUNCIL
of 9 March 1968

with a view to co-ordinating, in order to render of equal value the safeguards which Member States require of companies and firms within the meaning of the second paragraph of Article 58 of the Treaty, so as to protect the interests of both members and third parties.

This is the subject of this chapter. From now on I shall call it simply 'The first companies directive'. The official text of this instrument is at page L 65/8 of the *Journal Officiel* dated 14 March 1968 and bears the reference number 68/151/CEE.

At the time of writing there is no authentic English text. The text we have used in practice is the one produced by the translation service of the Foreign and Commonwealth Office. This is not yet on sale—but the Office have been good enough to allow me to reproduce it as Appendix 2 of this volume. I hope they will not think me ungrateful if, in discussing particular parts of the directive, I take the liberty of occasionally substituting my wording for theirs. My subject is, admittedly, a very thin slice of a very thick loaf; but there are two good reasons for this. In the first place, as this is the only piece of legislation which has been made on the subject of companies, it is the only one that has had to be considered with a view to changing our own law, and I know of nothing that so concentrates the mind of a civil service lawyer as the knowledge that he may have to prepare instructions to draft a Bill. The second reason is that it would be quite impossible to do justice to the complete range of measures projected in this field within the compass of one chapter. On the other hand, a brief account of those measures may not be inappropriate here, since it will give some idea of the range and nature of the material with which British company lawyers may have to grapple in the next few years.

THE COMPANY LAW PROGRAMME

These measures fall into three distinct groups: (1) draft directives under Article 54.2 and 54.3(*g*), (2) draft Conventions prepared for the purposes of Article 220, and (3) the project for a European company.

The directive I propose to consider deals with publicity, the validity of transactions entered into by a company, and nullity of companies. There are four other directives in various stages of preparation: one deals with company accounts; a second with the share capital, comprising such questions as the minimum capital with which a company can be incorporated, the reduction of capital, the effect of the loss of assets corresponding to the share capital; a third deals with internal mergers; a fourth with the structure of management and the powers of shareholders and of general meetings.

The draft Conventions prepared or being prepared for the purposes of Article 220 include one on the mutual recognition of firms and companies, another on the maintenance of legal personality in the event of transfer of the registered office from one country to another and a third on mergers of companies and firms subject to different domestic laws. Finally, there is the best known and most ambitious project of them all—the draft regulation relating to the setting up of a European company.

These are all important and interesting projects and when they materialise, as they will in the course of the next few years, they may present lawyers practising in this country with a wide and varied range of problems. They are, however, well beyond the modest scope of this chapter.

THE TREATY CONTEXT

It now becomes necessary, in order to try and assess the significance of the first companies directive, to say something about the legal framework within which it was made and within which it must operate. This involves a brief discussion of the provisions which indicate its purpose, the legal character of a 'directive' under the Treaty and the legal entities to which this directive applies.

The liberalisation of establishment. The directive forms part of a group of provisions made by and under the Treaty of Rome for the purpose of eliminating obstacles to the setting up of a common market. It is a commonplace that the removal of tariff barriers and import and export quotas is only a first step to the setting up of a common market. There are other obstacles: monopolies and restrictive practices are obvious examples, while technical differences in domestic laws relating to the composition, packaging, classification, description and performance of goods can, whether deliberately or not, prevent the free movement of goods between member States. The particular class of obstacle we are concerned with now is restrictions on the freedom of establishment of nationals of one member State in the territory of another member State. The expression 'freedom of establishment' probably has an unfamiliar 'continental' ring in the ears of an English lawyer. For the present purpose, however, it is enough to describe it as the freedom to settle in a country for the purpose of carrying on a business or profession there: this distinguishes it from the freedom of movement of workers on the one hand and the freedom to provide services on the other. How does the Treaty approach this problem and where do companies come in?

Part One of the Treaty ('Principles') provides in Article 3 that

> . . . the activities of the Community shall include, on the conditions and in accordance with the time-table provided in this Treaty . . .

(*c*) the abolition, as between Member States, of obstacles to freedom of movement for persons, services and capital.

Part Two deals, under four Titles, with the foundations of the Community: Title III deals, in four chapters, with the free movement of persons, services and capital; Chapter 1 of that Title deals with workers; Chapter 3 with services, and Chapter 4 with capital. Chapter 2 deals, in seven Articles (52–8), with the right of establishment.

The first companies directive was made under Article 54.2, 'in order to give effect to the general programme for the abolition of existing restrictions on freedom of establishment within the community, drawn up by the Council under [Article 54.1].' It was made in pursuance of the general requirement contained in Article 54.3(*g*), which requires the Council and the Commission to carry out the duties devolving upon them under Article 54.2,

in particular
(*g*) by co-ordinating to the necessary extent and rendering of equal value the guarantees which Member States require of companies and firms within the meaning of Article 58, second paragraph, so as to protect the interests of both shareholders and outsiders.

Legal character of a 'directive'. The legal instrument prescribed for the purpose of carrying out these programmes is the 'directive'. Article 189 of the Treaty provides that:

A directive shall be binding, as to the result to be achieved, upon each Member State to which it is directed, while leaving to national authorities the choice of form and methods.

A 'regulation', on the other hand,

Shall apply generally. It shall be binding in its entirety and take direct effect in each Member State.

A recent judgment of the European Court[1] indicates that the precise impact of any particular provision of secondary legislation is to be determined not by reference to the label attached to the instrument in which the provision appears but by reference to the character of the provision. You must therefore be prepared to find, in an instrument labelled 'directive', a provision which has direct effect in the territory of the member State concerned and, in an instrument labelled 'regulation', a provision which imposes obligations on a member State but does not have direct effect within its territory. This is something which may have to be borne in mind in examining the substantive provisions of future directives under this power—but it is doubtful if any part of the present directive can be regarded as having direct internal effect.

What conclusions can we draw from the choice of this type of instrument for implementing the programme for the liberalisation of establishment?

The most obvious, of course, is that it gives member States complete freedom to choose the method of carrying out their obligations: thus the United Kingdom would be free to use a statute, subordinate legislation under a statute or even a change in administrative practice—e.g. a change in licensing policy. The result is that an English legal adviser, studying the changes effected in implementation of a directive, would be concerned for the most part with the provisions of an English statute or statutory instrument, expressed in terms with which he is familiar, and hardly ever with the actual terms of the relevant Community law. I say 'hardly ever' because, as we shall see later, there are important, if rather vaguely defined limits to the powers under which the directive now in question was made. Cases may therefore arise in which an English lawyer might find it necessary before advising his client to refer to the terms of the directive. It might be *ultra vires*: this would not necessarily affect the validity under English law of the instrument made to implement it. If that instrument were a statute, the invalidity of the directive in Community law would probably not matter. If, on the other hand, it were a statutory instrument made under a power to implement directives—such a power might be regarded as a power to implement only directives valid under Community law. A further possibility is that a statutory instrument made to implement a directive might be open to challenge on the ground that it went further than was necessary for the purpose of implementing the directive in question. At the time of writing no one knows precisely how the statute or statutes necessary to enable the accession treaties to be ratified would deal with the problem: the two cases I have suggested illustrate the importance of making a close study of that enabling legislation even in this relatively narrow and technical field.

I must not stray too far from my chosen subject into the distinct but related subject of the system of judicial control which the Treaty of Rome has set up over its institutions;[2] but to complete the picture and to avoid misunderstanding I must make two brief comments. First, the English lawyer who was minded to challenge the validity of a directive would find at his disposal a far wider range of grounds for doing so than he finds in his own legal system. If you look at Article 173 you will find that they comprise 'lack of jurisdiction, infringements of important procedural rules, infringement of this Treaty or of any rule of law relating to its application or misuse of power'. Second, he would have no right of direct access to the European Court: he would have to persuade the appropriate English court to put the matter to the European Court under Article 177.[3]

The final conclusion to be drawn from the choice of the directive as the instrument for implementing the programme for liberalising establishment is that it is a clear indication of the limited and pragmatic character of the Treaty's approach to its appointed task. There is no question of setting up a new system of Community company law: all that is involved is a series of modifications of the company law of each member State to be effected by the institutions of that State and by the use of its own legal tools. So far as the directives contemplated under Articles 54.2 and 54.3(*g*) are concerned, the ultimate result will still be a body of independent national laws expressing their rules in their own traditional idiom but speaking a little less inconsistently in some respects than they did before. The draft regulation on the European company is, or may be, another story—but that I must not discuss here!

ANALYSIS OF ARTICLE 54.3(G)

Now is the time to look at the wording of Article 54.3(*g*), which prescribes how this type of directive is to serve the purpose of implementing the general programme on freedom of establishment. It is to do so 'by co-ordinating to the necessary extent and rendering of equal value the guarantees which Member States require of companies and firms within the meaning of Article 58, second paragraph', so as to protect the interests of both members and 'outsiders'. What are these 'guarantees'? What are 'companies and firms within the meaning of Article 58, second paragraph'? What precise shade of meaning are we to give to the word 'co-ordinating'? What authority determines the extent to which such co-ordination is 'necessary'?

The 'guarantees'. The great bulk of our company law consists of provisions ('guarantees') designed to protect investors and creditors—present and potential—from the risks implicit in incorporation, in the separation of ownership and management and in limited liability. In other words, the subject-matter of directives under Article 54.3(*g*) comprises almost the whole of our law relating to companies. It also covers a great part of the law relating to partnerships, but it seems that for some time this will be of no more than theoretical interest.

'Companies or firms'

Article 58.2 provides that:

> The term 'companies or firms' shall be understood to mean companies or firms constituted under civil or commercial law, including co-operative societies and other legal persons under public or private law save for non-profit-making companies or firms.

This formula contains some phrases unfamiliar to an English lawyer: 'civil or commercial', 'legal persons under public or private law'. For our present purposes we need not spend time analysing the difference between civil and commercial law or between public and private law. Under whichever system a 'company or firm' falls, it is caught. The expression 'companies or firms' is the current and quasi-official translation of the French *sociétés*. This word sets the trasnlator a difficult task—he must try to avoid using an English word which is either narrower or wider than the French word; or rather, than the French, German, Italian and Dutch words. This is all the more difficult because, certainly in English, and I suspect in French too, we are dealing with words which cannot be precisely defined, and which owe their current meaning to the legal and commercial development of the last 150 years. To our ears the phrase 'companies or firms' tends to convey the meaning 'bodies corporate or partnerships'—but if you look again at the wording of Article 58.2 you see the words 'and other legal persons . . .', which seems to exclude unincorporated partnerships. This is not necessarily conclusive. When the European lawyer talks about 'other legal persons' I suspect he is not using a scientific formula but a label to describe those associations which under his law are regarded as having legal personality and have the historical characteristics of a *société*. We in this country certainly have not equated 'company' with 'body corporate'; the historical subject-matter of our companies legislation is the unincorporated trading company which emerged during the early nineteenth century and differed from a traditional partnership in two respects: the member's freedom to transfer his shares without the consent of his fellow members, and the separation of ownership and management. The registered company of today is more than a mere body corporate, it is still in principle a voluntary association upon which there have been superimposed the attributes of a body corporate. The Coal Board is a body corporate, it is not a company. To paraphrase Maitland's famous epigram, the old unincorporated company continues to rule us from its grave. I do not want to ride this hobby-horse too long, but I think a good case could be made out for saying that the history of company law for the last forty years shows a gradual process of correcting the anomalies that flowed from a failure to realise that a 'company' is more than a mere body corporate. I have dwelt on this theme at some length because I think it important to establish that what we are faced with in Article 58.2 is a group of persons in voluntary association for the purpose of carrying on a business for gain. This is far from being a theoretical matter, as I shall try to make clear when we come to look at the problem of adapting the first company directive so as to apply it intelligibly to our system of company law.

'Co-ordinating'

The precise meaning of this word has been the subject of much argument—some of it of almost theological subtlety. It is also of some practical importance, because Article 100 of the Treaty gives the Council a very wide power to issue directives 'for the approximation of such provisions imposed by the law, regulation and administrative action in Member States as directly affect the setting up or operation of the Common Market'. 'Approximation' under Article 100 requires a unanimous decision at all times; 'co-ordination' can be achieved after the first stage by a qualified majority. Whatever may be the precise difference between co-ordination and approximation, it is clear that the purpose of the two provisions is quite different. The purpose of Article 100 is to eliminate obstacles: the purpose of Article 54.3(*g*) is strictly complementary to the process of liberating establishment; in other words, it is designed to enable the Council to avoid or reduce the dangers and distortions involved in the process of liberalising establishment. It is not intended to enable the Council to start *unifying* the company law of the member States.

'To the extent necessary'

There is little doubt that the European Court would put an objective interpretation on these words. They therefore operate as a very effective curb on the use of the power. That is not to say that there are likely to be many successful challenges to the *vires* of this type of directive; the elaborate process of consultation that has to be completed before a directive is finally agreed upon should almost always ensure that no directive is made under this power unless it is demonstrably necessary for the purpose outlined in the previous paragraph.

'Companies or firms' as 'nationals'

What Article 52 requires to be abolished is 'restrictions on the freedom of establishment of *nationals* of a Member State' (my italics). Article 58.1 tells us that 'companies or firms' formed in accordance with the law of a member State and having their registered office, central administration or principal place of business within the Community shall, for the purposes of [Chapter 2, comprising Articles 52–8], be treated in the same way as natural persons who are nationals of member States. The 'companies or firms' which are the beneficiaries of the various directives liberalising establishment in the various classes of occupation also include 'companies or firms set up in conformity with the law of an overseas country or territory [as to which see Article 131 of the Treaty of Rome] and having their registered office, central administration or principal place of business within the Community or in an overseas country or territory'; in order to benefit from the directives both classes of company, if they have only a registered office within the Community or an overseas country or territory, must show that 'their business activity has a continuous and effective link with the economy of a Member State or of an overseas country or territory'.

THE TERMS OF THE DIRECTIVE—THE PREAMBLE

We can now look at the terms of the first companies directive. The preamble is instructive; it tells us in general terms (*a*) what kind of company is being dealt with, (*b*) what matters are being dealt with in relation to those companies, and (*c*) why. Two kinds of company are affected—the official translation prudently reproduces the French text with an English paraphrase; the companies concerned are (*a*) 'sociétés par actions' and (*b*) 'sociétés à responsabilité limitée'. Here we seem to be faced at once with a problem of classification; under our system companies with a share capital and companies with limited liability are not mutually exclusive categories. But if we look at the reason given for dealing with these companies, I think it becomes reasonably clear that this theoretical problem must not be taken too seriously. These companies have been chosen because they are companies which frequently carry on business 'beyond their national frontiers'. This gives us a first, very general clue to the sort of United Kingdom company the directive would have to cover if it were to impose the same obligations on us as it does on the existing members of the Six. It is those companies which are most likely to take early advantage of the freedom to establish in other countries of the Community.

ARTICLE 1. TYPES OF COMPANY AFFECTED

Looking now at the operative words of the directive, we find in Article 1 that each country is told to which of the various types of company that can be formed under its law the directive applies. Two types of company are common to all the existing members: they are the German *Aktiengesellschaft* and the *Kommanditgesellschaft auf Atkien* and their equivalents in Belgium, France, Italy, Luxembourg and the Netherlands. The directive also applies to the German *Gesellschaft mit beschränkter Haftung* and its equivalents in every country of the Six except Holland—Dutch law apparently does not provide for this type of company.

What are the essential characteristics of these companies? For our purposes they can be summarised as follows:

1. They are all what we should call 'bodies corporate'; for the purposes of this directive we do not therefore pursue any further the general question posed by Article 58.2 whether a *société* includes an unincorporated partnership.
2. They are—in principle, at any rate—more than mere 'bodies corporate'; they are incorporated 'companies'.
3. The members are incorporated on the footing that they are to be liable for or in respect of the debts of the body corporate.
4. Liability is limited.
5. They must pursue a 'but lucratif'. The current F.C.O. version translates this as 'profit-making': this seems to be too narrow.

'Having for their object the acquisition of gain by the company or by the members thereof' is probably nearer to the French.
6. They are creatures of 'private', not 'public', law.

How can we most simply describe the United Kingdom companies which satisfy both the general description in the preamble and the specific requirements set out above? At the time of writing this has not yet been finally agreed, but we can be reasonably happy that the directive would have the same practical effect on our law as it now does on the laws of the Six if it is adapted to apply to 'companies incorporated with limited liability'.

The bodies to which the directive need *not* apply are unlimited companies, unincorporated partnerships or associations, bodies which by their constitution are inhibited from carrying on business for gain—of the body itself or its members—industrial and provident societies and building societies, and those bodies which are now loosely described as 'public corporations', ranging from the Coal Board, the B.B.C., the National Research and Development Corporation and the Cotton Board. Whether and to what extent there might be advantages in modifying our law so as to bring some of these bodies within the scope of the implementing legislation is another matter.

The requirements imposed by the directive relate to 'publicity', 'the validity of transactions entered into by the company' and 'the nullity of companies'. I propose to say nothing about the last beyond this, that 'nullity' appears to be a phenomenon peculiar to French and Belgian company law. The provisions of Part III, which deal with nullity, may be of interest to the British resident who invests in or gives credit to a French company but its impact on the company law of the United Kingdom would apparently be nil. (To avoid confusion I use the word 'part' in preference to the word 'section' used in the official translation to describe the main divisions of the directive.)

Part I

'Publicity' is covered by Part I, which comprises Articles 1–6. Article 2 tells us what is to be made public; Article 3 tells us how; Article 4 deals with the particulars to be given on letter headings and order forms; Article 5 requires member States to determine the persons who are required to effect publication. Article 6 requires penalties to be prescribed for the breach of any obligations imposed in pursuance of Articles 2.1(*f*) and 4.

I propose to discuss only those matters which would involve changes in our law or seem to call for some elucidation.

Article 2.1(*c*) requires an amended version of the memorandum and articles or their equivalent to be made public after each alteration.

Article 2.1(*d*) requires publication of particulars of the appointment, vacation of office and names of people described as 'organs' and having the functions described in heads (i) and (ii). (As I shall try to explain later when discussing Part II, these 'organs' are not as unfamiliar to us as they may seem at first sight.)

Article 2.1(*f*) requires the balance sheet to indicate the identity of the persons who are required by law to 'certify' it. This is intended to refer to the auditors—although our Companies Act does not, strictly speaking, require them to 'certify' accounts. Section 127 of the Companies Act, 1948, effectively complies with this requirement.

The requirements of Article 2.1(*f*) apply to the *Gesellschaft mit beschränkter Haftung* or its equivalents in the other member States until a further directive is issued co-ordinating their laws on accounts and making an exception in favour of companies with assets below a prescribed balance sheet value. That directive has not yet been made, although it is overdue. So far as England and Scotland are concerned, this is not of immediate interest, since the special privileges of the exempt private company were abolished by the Companies Act, 1967. They are of interest to Northern Ireland, where the Companies Act still exempts the private company from having to annex its balance sheet and profit and loss account to its annual return. The exemption contemplated in the proposed directive might well be of interest to England and Scotland if the Companies Acts, 1948 and 1967, were amended to relieve small companies from the obligation to publish their accounts. Paragraph 2 is instructive; the law of Holland does not provide for the *Gesellschaft mit beschränkter Haftung* of German law or the S.A.R.L. of French law. The draftsman has therefore been compelled to define it in general terms. It corresponds roughly to our private company, but the definition is noticeably tighter than section 28 of our Companies Act.

Article 2.1(*h*) is aimed at those countries which, unlike us, dissolve and then wind up.

Article 2.1(*j*) does not involve any change in our practice: the powers of our liquidators under sections 245(1) and (2) and 303(1) are all derived expressly and exclusively from the Companies Act, even though some of them may be exercised only with prescribed consents.

Article 3 tells us how the information specified in Article 2 is to be made available to the public.

Article 3.2 gives member States a choice between the 'filing' and 'registration' systems. This would involve no change in our system, under which the so-called 'register' is in fact a series of files.

Article 3.3 requires the information specified in Article 2 to be available on payment of a charge not exceeding cost. This looks very like section 426 of the Companies Act, 1948. Section 426 does not mention requests by post—but it is the Registrar's practice to supply copies of documents against requests by post: this is a good example of an obligation imposed by a directive being discharged by administrative practice without any specific provision in the law.

Article 3.4 would have the effect of requiring all information registered under Article 2 to be noted or reproduced in the London, Edinburgh and Belfast *Gazettes*. The burden would, of course be much heavier here than it is in any of the other member States. Here it would affect something like 450,000 companies: in West Germany the number of *Aktiengesellschaften* existing in April 1967 was only 2,500; and the number of G.m.b.H.'s 54,000. Some critics have been saying for years that we make registration under the Companies Act altogether too easy and that we should provide a simple form of incorporation for what are essentially small partnerships.

Articles 3.5 and 3.7 would effect an important change in our law. Article 3.6 would operate only in the somewhat unlikely event of our deciding to require all documents filed and information furnished under Article 2 to be reproduced in full in the *Gazettes*. Under Article 3.5 a third party is not affected by notice of any information required to be registered by Article 2 until it has been notified in the *Gazette* unless the company can show that he had actual notice of it. The third party enjoys the additional safeguard that, as regards transactions entered into before the sixteenth day after the date of notification in the *Gazette*, he is not affected by notice if he can show that he could not have seen the notification. A third party, however, can rely on a legal act that has not been registered, unless it is invalid for lack of registration.

It would be wrong to say that the introduction of civil as distinct from penal sanctions for failure to register would be a complete novelty in our law, but this provision of the directive carries the principle much further than we have ever done in this field.

Its practical effect will be important. To take two examples: (*a*) a change of directors, and (*b*) a change in the situation of the registered office. Section 200(4) of the Companies Act, 1948, requires changes among a company's directors to be notified to the Registrar of Companies. Section 107 requires notice of any change in the situation of the registered office to be notified to the Registrar. In neither case does the Act say that a third party is not to be affected by the change until it has been registered. Article 3.5 would apparently have that effect.

Article 4 requires the company's letters and forms to state

> [the situation of] a registry at which the file required by Article 3 is available for inspection and the registration number of the company in that register, the legal character of the company, the situation of its registered office and (if applicable) its current state of liquidation.

If any such document refers to the capital of the company, both the amount issued and the amount paid up must be stated. The breach of this obligation does not involve any civil consequences but Article 6 requires sanctions to be provided, as it also does for failure to publish accounts as required by Article 2.

Part II

Article 7 expresses the rule in *Kelner* v. *Baxter* (1866), L.R. 2 C.P., except that it seems to be neutral on the question of ratification.

Articles 8 and 9 are probably the most interesting and important provisions of this directive. The problems they are concerned with are, of course, familiar—but the solutions they provide would involve important changes in our law. The first problem is essentially to determine who 'represents' the company in transactions with third parties. The next is to determine what are the limits to the representatives' power to bind the company.

German law gives a clear and uncompromising answer to these questions. For the sake of simplicity, I will confine myself to the position of the *Aktiengesellschaft*. Every such company must have a *Vorstand* to manage its affairs and the *Vorstand* represents the company both before the courts and in all other transactions with the outside world. (*Vorstand* is usually translated as 'board of management'; a more precise, if somewhat pedantic, translation would be 'organ of management', since the *Vorstand* can consist of only one person.) Next, Article 82 of the *Aktiengesetz* of 1965 provides in unqualified terms that the authority of the *Vorstand* to represent the association may not be limited; this is carried to its logical conclusion—the company may not escape from obligations accepted by the *Vorstand* either on the ground that the *Vorstand* exceeded his authority or on the ground that the transaction was *ultra vires* the company.

Section 176 of the Companies Act, 1948, requires every private company and every company registered before 1 November 1929 to have at least one director, and every other company to have two.

The Act does not state expressly what the powers of the directors are—that is left to the articles. It does impose duties and liabilities on the directors, and for this purpose a director includes not only a person formally appointed to that office but any person who 'occupies the position of director by whatever name called'. Nor does it tell us who has the power to represent the company in transactions with the outside world. The courts originally answered this question by reference to the law of agency: the inadequacy of this explanation is very clearly spelled out in chapters 7 and 8 of the third edition of Gower's *Modern Company Law*. The courts have recognised the need to find what Lord Haldane called 'the directing mind and will of the corporation', in other words, an organ which acts as the company and not merely as its agent. This is the organ which can bind the company in transactions with third parties—generally the directors acting collegiately. But there are two further questions that the third party has to answer before he can deal with the officers of a company in the confidence that they can bind it. 'Is the transaction within the power of the company?' 'Is it within the apparent authority of the person I am dealing with?' If the answer to either question is 'no' then the company is not bound.

Here the directive comes down firmly in favour of the third party. Article 9.1 would require the abrogation of our *ultra vires* rule. The company is bound to third parties by transactions entered into by its organs even if those transactions are outside the objects of the company. This is qualified by paragraph 2, which permits (but does not *require*) member States to provide that a company shall not be bound by a transaction which the third party knew (or in all the circumstances could not have been ignorant) was not within the company's objects.

Even if a member State takes advantage of this qualification, it *may not* provide that publication of the memorandum and articles constitutes notice. This would involve important changes in our law; but they are changes that most academic and many practising lawyers have been demanding for many years, and indeed the compromise which Article 9.1 permits is almost exactly what the Jenkins Committee recommended at paragraph 42 of their report.[4] Jenkins also recommended that actual notice of the memorandum and articles should not deprive a third party of his right to enforce the contract if he honestly and reasonably failed to appreciate that they precluded the company or its officers from entering into the contract; this goes beyond the requirements of the directive, but as those requirements represent the minimum protection which member States must give to their third parties there is nothing in the directive which would prevent us from implementing it.

The powers of the directors are, of course, not to be absolutely unlimited: some restrictions are imposed by law and they continue to limit the directors' powers and therefore the company's liability: for example, an agreement by the directors to issue shares to X when the authorised capital of the company has already been fully issued would plainly be unenforceable against the company, whatever remedy X might have against the directors.

Article 9.2 treats contracts made in excess of the directors' powers but within the objects of the company in the same way: such contracts might still be attacked on the ground that they were fraudulent to the knowledge of the third party.

Section 9.3 provides for those member States whose laws, although they vest the power of external representation in the 'organ of management', permit the 'statutes' of a company to derogate from the general rule by vesting that power either in an individual or in each of a number of individuals or in a number of individuals acting jointly. The situation contemplated by this provision seems to arise only when the person or body in whom the power would otherwise be vested is deprived of it: thus Article 78(3) of the German *Aktiengesetz* of 1965 permits the articles of association to determine that individual members of the board may be given the power to represent the company [solely, or jointly with a *Prokurist*]; but this power is in addition to, and not in derogation from, the power conferred upon the *Vorstand* by Article 78(1) of that law, and Article 9.3 of the directive therefore does not apply.

A case in which it would apply is where the articles of a Belgian *société de personnes à responsabilité limitée* provide that the power of external representation should be vested in two *gérants* acting jointly. The general rule appears to be that this power is vested in any one of the *gérants* acting alone: the articles therefore derogate from the general rule, and Article 9.3 of the directive does apply.

When it does apply, it expressly reserves the right of the country concerned to permit the company to rely on that provision against third parties. Thus, if a third party purports to contract with the company through a person or body in which the general law would vest the power of representation, the company can repudiate the contract on the ground that its articles had deprived that person or body of that power. The company may be permitted to do this. however, only on two conditions. First, the power thus vested must be the *general* power of representation. Second, the requirements of Article 3 on publicity must be complied with. In other words, the company must have taken the prescribed steps to warn the third party by publishing the right information in the right place and in good time. This accounts for the detailed information about the 'organ of management' required by Article 2.1(*d*).

How would these provisions affect our law? The general rule is that a board of directors exercises its powers, including the power of external representation, collectively: but a registered company may provide for this power to be vested in an individual director or directors or in a committee of directors to the exclusion of the board. This is clearly a situation to which Article 9.3 applies. The company would not be able to rely any longer on the fact that articles are a public document: section 200(4) of the Companies Act would need to be expanded as required by Article 2.1(*d*), and express provision would seem to be necessary about the effect of a failure to register on the rights of third parties.

CONCLUSIONS

It might be convenient if I now indicated a few general conclusions that I think we can draw from this study of the first companies directive. These can be summarised as follows:

1. There is no question yet of introducing a common code of Community company law into the laws of member States; these

directives would require changes in our law which would be implemented by familiar instruments expressing familiar ideas in familiar language if we did join the Common Market.

2. Even the first companies directive, however, could involve recourse to the system of judicial control over legislative and administrative organs of the Community which is incorporated in the Treaty of Rome.
3. The essential purpose of the directive is to ensure that each member State shall provide substantially the same measure of protection for potential and actual investors, and creditors, actual and potential.
4. If we accede to the Community, our company law would have to be altered by abolishing the *ultra vires* rule and the rule that third parties dealing with a company are deemed to have notice of any limits imposed on the powers of directors by its memorandum and articles.
5. There would be an appreciable increase in the amount of information to be made public by companies; this would involve a considerable burden on company secretaries and possibly—but this depends on decisions not yet taken—the staff of the Registrar of Companies.
6. Generally, the trend of the directive is to tilt the balance firmly in favour of a third party dealing with a company and to provide explicitly for matters which we have long tended to take for granted, e.g. the question whether the board of directors must act collectively to bind the company.
7. These are all changes which reformers in this country have been demanding for years. There is nothing doctrinaire, exotic or 'foreign' about them.

NOTES

[1] *Transports Lesage & Cie.* v. *Hauptzollamt Fribourg, Recueil de la jurisprudence,* 1970, p. 861, [1971] C.M.L.R. 1.

[2] See Chapter V, at p. 57.

[3] See *ibid.* at p. 60.

[4] Cmnd. 1749.

ACKNOWLEDGMENT

I should like to express my gratitude to the University of Manchester for the honour they did me in inviting me to give the lecture which formed the substance of this chapter, and to the Department of Trade and Industry for authorising me to accept the invitation.

Chapter V

THE COURT OF JUSTICE OF THE EUROPEAN COMMUNITIES

Gillian White

CREATION AND ROLE OF THE COURT

A good starting point when describing any institution is perhaps to ask the simple question 'Why was it created?' Or, to put it another way, 'What function is it intended to fulfil?' So far as the Court of Justice is concerned, the answer given in the treaties setting up the three European Communities is expressed in a single sentence. Article 164 of the E.E.C. Treaty provides: 'The Court of Justice shall ensure that the law is observed in the interpretation and implementation of this Treaty.'[1]

The present Court succeeded to the original Court of Justice of the European Coal and Steel Community in October 1958. The creation of that Court in 1952 was an action of very great legal and political significance. Judge Donner, who was the first President of the new Court from 1958 to 1964, has written:

> By providing it with a Court of Justice, the founders of the European Coal and Steel Community, set up in 1952, stressed the novel and serious nature of their undertaking. The Community was not to be just an international body, subject, like so many others, to the hazards of international diplomacy. It would be an independent entity with its own laws and entering, without having to seek the approval of the contracting States, into a direct legal relationship with its own subjects, the coal and steel concerns in the member States.[2]

Judge Donner went on to observe that the movement towards European integration had suffered some disillusionment by 1958, resulting in various modifications to the institutional structure in the E.E.C. and Euratom Treaties compared with the Coal and Steel Treaty.

> But that distinctive feature of supra-nationalism, an independent and powerful European judiciary, had already established itself firmly enough to be extended to the new Communities without discussion and with only minor changes. It was decided not to triple the judicial institution of the three Communities, but to give all three a single Court and

to merge the Coal and Steel Court into the judicial authorities established by the Rome Treaties.[3]

The Court has a wide range of jurisdiction under the treaties, some aspects of which will be examined in this lecture. The law which it is to apply is not laid down in any provision comparable to Article 38 of the Statute of the International Court of Justice. It has to interpret and apply the treaties themselves, which to a large extent are statements of economic principles and objectives rather than legal propositions. It has also to interpret the extensive and complicated 'subsidiary legislation' made by the Council or the Commission under their treaty powers. It has to control the legality of the exercise of those same powers, by reference to standards and concepts taken from the administrative law of the six countries, principally from French administrative law. This is not an exhaustive list, but it gives an idea of the creative role entrusted to the Court. For, as Wall has expressed it, 'the case law it develops takes its place alongside the Treaties as the law of the Communities'.[4]

THE SINGLE COURT

The single Court for the three Communities was set up by Articles 3 and 4 of a Convention concluded at the same time as the Treaty of Rome, entitled 'Convention relating to Certain Institutions common to the European Communities'.[5] Article 3 provides that the jurisdiction conferred upon the Court of Justice by the E.E.C. Treaty and by the Euratom Treaty shall be exercised by a single court of justice, but 'under the conditions respectively laid down in those treaties'. Article 4 provides for the dissolution of the Coal and Steel Community Court and its replacement by the single Court which is to exercise the Coal and Steel Court's jurisdiction in accordance with the provisions of the E.C.S.C. Treaty

COMPOSITION

The composition of the Court and the appointment of the Judges, the Advocates-General, the Registrar and other officials, are dealt with in identical articles in the E.E.C. and Euratom Treaties.[6] The qualifications for the Judges and for the Advocates-General are identical. They must be

> persons whose independence can be fully relied upon and who fulfil the conditions required for the exercise of the highest Court functions

in their respective countries or who are legal experts of universally recognised ability.[7]

There is no provision for 'national judges', and it would be possible to have more than two from a particular member State, leaving another member with no Judge of its own nationality, but this is unlikely to occur because appointment is by common agreement among all the member governments.[8] The treaties provide for a Court of seven Judges, which has been applied in practice to give one Judge from each State, with a seventh Judge from any of the States. The present composition of the Court is

Robert Lecourt (France), *President*
Andreas Donner (Netherlands)
J. Mertens de Wilmars (Belgium)
Riccardo Monaco (Italy)
Pierre Pescatore (Luxembourg)
Hans Kutscher (Germany)
Alberto Trabucchi (Italy)

An increase in the number of Judges, which will be needed for the new member States, is effected by unanimous decision of the Council at the request of the Court.[9]

ADVOCATES-GENERAL

The treaties provide that the Court 'shall be assisted' by two Advocates-General.[10] Their office and task are unfamiliar to common lawyers. As stated, their qualifications are precisely the same as those of the Judges themselves; the Advocates-General take the same oath, enjoy the same immunity and are subject to the same obligations not to hold any political or administrative office or engage in any paid or unpaid occupation while they hold office as Advocates-General.[11] Their task, as laid down in the treaties, is

> to make reasoned submissions in open Court, with complete impartiality and independence, on cases submitted to the Court of Justice, with a view to assisting the Court in the performance of the duty assigned to it in Article 164.[12]

Most commentators have regarded their role as closely comparable to that of the *Commissaires du gouvernement* at the French Conseil d'Etat.[13] But Judge Donner considers that they resemble more nearly the *Ministères publics* of the courts of cassation known to several of the six member countries.[14] These are officials who, in France, exercise a general supervision over the administration of civil justice, in addition to their duties as prosecutors. They are under the direction of the Minister of Justice and themselves comprise the *Ministère Public*. They have a right to be heard in all cases in the French *Cour de cassation* and in many categories of cases in other courts, including cases affecting public order, the State, public authorities and cases of personal status.[15] In the courts of cassation the *Ministères publics* have to present impartial conclusions on questions of law and fact raised by each case. The courts must consider these conclusions but is not bound to follow them.

Judge Donner has emphasised the value and importance of the Advocates-General for the European Court, which is not an appellate court[16] and from which there is no appeal. Supreme courts in national jurisdiction have the advantage of argument before the lower courts and, usually, of the reasoned judgments of these courts.[17]

PROCEDURE OF THE COURT

This is not the place to give an account of the procedure of the European Court. Excellent and detailed works on this in English have already been published.[18] The British practitioner[19] will have to adapt to an unfamilar mode in which the Court exercises considerable initiative in investigating the facts in dispute as well as researching into the law. If the Court decides that an 'Instruction' is necessary in a particular case, the Court will decide what witnesses are to be summoned, and will play a leading part in examining the witnesses. The Court can request parties to produce documents and information, and it can order expert reports. Wall has suggested that this procedure reflects the concern with powers, as distinct from rights, which has characterised administrative courts in many European systems. He points out that it has long been customary for such courts to take upon themselves much of the necessary investigation and inquiry in their review of the legality of the exercise of governmental powers.[20]

The other distinctive feature of the Court's procedure when looked at with British eyes is the predominant importance of written briefs and argument over oral argument. As regards the language of the proceedings, it is for the plaintiff to choose one of the four official languages, French, German, Italian or Dutch. The defendant, usually a Community institution, must then reply in this language, which becomes the 'language of procedure' (*langue de procédure*). Thus equal access to the Court for parties from any member State is assured.[21] However, when the defendant is a member State, as in proceedings brought by the Commission for alleged failure to perform the E.E.C. Treaty, under Article 169,[22] the plaintiff Commission uses the language of the defendant State —a courteous bow in the direction of national tradition which indicates awareness of the political sensitivity that may accompany cases under Article 169. Most of the Judges are fluent in at least one of the official languages in addition to their mother tongue. Simultaneous translation of oral argument is provided for them, as are translations of the written briefs. These services are provided from the Court's budget and are not paid for by the parties.[23] Judgment will be given in the language of procedure for that case, and translated into the other three languages by the Court's staff. Official reports are published in all four languages.

The European Court is faithful to Continental legal tradition in that it delivers a single judgment in each case, with no individual opinions or dissenting judgments. If one or more Judges do not agree with the majority, this is never disclosed. Undoubtedly much of the strength of the Court as the guardian of Community law and as an instrument for its development is attributable to this single judgment.

JURISDICTION

Within this short compass one cannot hope to expound all the bases of jurisdiction given to the Court by the three treaties, nor go into detail about the types of case that are brought under these different provisions. The literature is already extensive and much of it is in English—more, one suspects, for the American reader than for British lawyers, but this is rapidly changing.

It is as well to be clear from the outset that the European Court does not have exclusive jurisdiction over all disputes and matters arising under the treaties or under other Community legislation. The treaties and the legislation create many rights and duties which are cognisable and enforceable by national courts of the member States. Moreover, the Communities have legal personality, and legal capacity to sue or be sued in these courts.[24] This concurrence of jurisdiction is expressed in Article 183 of the E.E.C. Treaty:

> Subject to the powers conferred on the Court of Justice by this Treaty, cases to which the Community is a party shall not for that reason alone be excluded from the jurisdiction of the domestic courts or tribunals of Member States.

It is also reflected in a fundamental article, Article 177, providing for reference to the European Court for a preliminary ruling upon questions of the interpretation of the Treaty, or the validity and interpretation of measures of the Community institutions. Article 177, on which there is already a considerable body of case law, both of the European Court and of national courts, and a growing body of literature, will be discussed later in this chapter.

Having this concurrence of jurisdiction in mind, we can mention some of the heads of jurisdiction of the European Court, taking the E.E.C. Treaty only, and ignoring for reasons of space the E.C.S.C. Treaty and those few provisions of the Euratom Treaty which differ from those of the E.E.C. Treaty

BREACH OF THE TREATY

An alleged failure by a member State to fulfil any of its obligations under the Treaty may be brought to the Court by the Commission under Article 169, or by another member State under Article 170. So far, member States have not used this jurisdiction against each other, but the Commission has brought numerous cases under Article 169. Many more potential disputes between the Commission and a member State have been settled by negotiation. This is facilitated by the requirement that the State must be given the opportunity to submit its comments to the Commission, which then, if it still considers that the State is in breach, must issue a 'reasoned opinion' on the matter, giving the State a period for compliance. Other member States are entitled to intervene in such cases,[25] and have made full use of this right. In this way Article 169 provides an effective means for a member State to present submissions to the Court concerning acts or omissions by another member which it considers amount to failure to perform the Treaty, without having to 'accuse' that fellow member directly. Should the Court find that a member State has failed to fulfil a Treaty obligation, it may order the State to take whatever measures are required to remedy the situation—for example, amendment or repeal of legislation.[26]

It has bee nobserved that proceedings under Article 169 are 'the final stage of what is usually a long-lasting dispute between a member State and the Commission'.[27] Moreover, the 'failure' by the State may well stem from a genuine difference of opinion on the interpretation or application of Community law, and is not to be thought of necessarily as a deliberate breach of the Treaty.

CONTROL OF LEGALITY OF MEASURES

Member States have rights of recourse to the Court to challenge the legality of measures taken by the Council or the Commission on the four grounds of lack of competence (*ultra vires*); breach of important procedural provisions; breach of the Treaty or breach of any rule relating to its application; or misuse of power (*détournement de pouvoir*). These rights of challenge, conferred by Article 173, give the Court its celebrated and vital function of judicial review or control of the legality of Community legislation. The institutions themselves, Council and Commission, have identical rights of recourse to the Court to challenge each other's measures. Individuals, firms, companies and other legal persons have a much more limited right of challenge, based on the same four grounds, but restricted to individual decisions directed to them. It should be noted that there is a two-month limitation period for proceedings under Article 173. This applies irrespective of whether the plaintiff is a government, an institution or an individual.

The Court has developed a considerable jurisprudence on the four grounds of challenge, which were based on European administrative law, particularly French law.[28] Community measures found by the Court to be illegal on any of the four grounds are quashed by declaration of the Court.[29]

Member States may also complain to the Court if the Council or the Commission omits to take action in circumstances in which omission violates the Treaty.[30] The institutions may similarly bring each other's omissions before the Court. If the Court quashes an illegal measure, under Article 174, or declares an omission to be in violation of the Treaty, the institution responsible must take the necessary action to comply with the judgment.[31]

PROTECTION OF INDIVIDUALS AND COMPANIES

So far as companies, firms or individuals are concerned, the judicial review provisions of Articles 173 and 175 are so restricted as to be of limited value as a protection against unlawful acts by the Council or Commission.[32] Their protection is contained rather in Articles 172 and 184, indirectly in preliminary references under Article 177, and in proceedings brought by the member States under the provisions we have just considered. Article 172 is an enabling provision by which regulations of the Council may confer plenary jurisdiction (*pleine juridiction*) on the Court in regard to the penalties laid down in such regulations. Thus a company which is fined by the Commission for some agreement or practice contrary to the regulations on competition may appeal to the Court against the decision imposing the fine. It can do so because Regulation No. 17 on competition conferred plenary jurisdiction on the Court. The individual *decision* can be challenged on the ground that the penalty is not due—for instance, because the restrictive agreement has been modified,[33] or on the ground that the fine is excessive. It can also be challenged on any of the four grounds in Article 173, if appropriate. If the company wishes to contest the applicability of Regulation No. 17 itself to the facts, it may do so under Article 184. But Article 184 does not provide a means of leaping over the restrictions placed upon appeals by companies or individuals in Article 173. It simply enables the plea that a regulation is inapplicable to be made in proceedings based on some other article of the Treaty, for example an appeal to the plenary jurisdiction (*en pleine juridiction*) under Article 172.[34]

ENFORCEMENT OF THE COURT'S JUDGMENTS[58]

All three treaties deal with this matter in the same way, with the result that no provision concerning the judgments of the Court or their enforcement was needed in the Convention on Institutions common to the European Communities.[35]

Article 187 of the E.E.C. Treaty provides:

> The judgments of the Court of Justice shall be enforceable under the conditions laid down in Article 192.

Article 192 in turn provides:

> Decisions of the Council or of the Commission which involve a pecuniary obligation on persons other than States, shall have the enforceability of a Court Judgment.

Enforcement shall be governed by the rules of civil procedure in force in the State in the territory of which it takes place. The order for its enforcement shall be appended to the decision, without other formality than verification of the authenticity of the decision, by the national authority which the Government of each Member State shall designate for this purpose and shall make known to the Commission and to the Court of Justice.

When these formalities have been completed at request, the party concerned may proceed to enforcement by bringing the matter directly before the authority which is competent according to the law of the country concerned.

Enforcement may be suspended only by a decision of the Court of Justice. The propriety of methods [of] enforcement, however, shall be a matter for the courts of the country concerned.

This article is more clearly drafted than the corresponding provision in the Coal and Steel Treaty, Article 92, and the last sentence on the national court's control of methods of enforcement, does not appear in the earlier treaty.

The effect of Article 192[36] is to confer upon the record of a decision in any case the status of an exequatur or formal statement of authenticity thereof.[37] The designated national authority will merely have to see that this complies with Article 64(2) of the rules of procedure of the Court:

The original record of the judgment, signed by the President, by the Judges who took part in the consideration of the judgment [*délibéré*] and by the Registrar, shall be sealed and deposited in the Registrar's office; a certified copy of it shall be sent to each of the parties.

When this has been done the pecuniary sum due will be enforced in the same way as a judgment under a Convention made pursuant to the Foreign Judgments (Reciprocal Enforcement) Act, 1933.[59]

Costs of execution in any State are payable by the party against whom the judgment is enforced, according to the scale of costs in force in the State where enforcement takes place.[38]

The type of judgment to which these provisions relate is a judgment for damages, for example, in an action brought against the Community, sued in the person of the Commission for liability under Articles 178 and 215.[39] Execution against the property or assets of the Community, if matters ever reached that stage, would be subject to any relevant immunity under Article 218 and the Protocol on Privileges and Immunities. Other judgments of the Court do not need to be enforced by any special procedure but bear their own executory force. For example, if a State is found by the Court to be in breach of a treaty obligation, it may be ordered by the Court to take the necessary remedial action.[40] In the most unlikely event of a government refusing to do so, the Court has no 'sanction' under the Rome treaties. Under the Coal and Steel Treaty the defaulting member State can be fined, in effect, by a decision of the High Authority with the agreement of the Council deciding by a two-thirds majority. Sums due to that State by the High Authority may then be withheld.[41] But we are here positing a situation of confrontation between member State and Court which could be resolved only by political agreement and for which strictly legal remedies are not yet suited, given the present stage of development of the Communities.

Finally, it is appropriate to mention again, in this context, that a declaration by the Court that a Community measure, such as a regulation or decision, is illegal operates to quash that measure.[42] The institution responsible must take the necessary steps to comply with the judgment. This applies both to the quashing of an illegal act and to a declaration by the Court that the institution's failure to act is contrary to the Treaty.[43] Regulations, however, are severable. The Court may indicate 'which of the effects of the regulation which it has quashed shall be regarded as confirmed'.[44]

CO-OPERATION WITH NATIONAL COURTS

References under Article 177

A feature of the Court's work in the last two or three years has been the sharp increase in the number of preliminary references by national courts under Article 177. In 1970 thirty-two cases were begun under Article 177, compared with seventeen such cases begun in 1969. The present position seems to be that about one case in every three on the Court's list is a preliminary reference. This marked trend, in comparison with the type of case brought in the earlier years of the Court's life, reflects the growing impact of Community law upon the national law of the member countries. National courts are more and more obliged to apply and so to interpret Community law.[45]

Article 177 provides:

> The Court of Justice shall have jurisdiction to give preliminary rulings concerning:

(*a*) the interpretation of this Treaty;
(*b*) the validity and interpretation of measures taken by the institutions of the Community;
(*c*) the interpretation of the statutes of bodies set up by a formal measure of the Council, where those statutes so provide.

Where such a question is raised before any court or tribunal of one of the Member States, that court or tribunal may, if it considers that a decision on the question is necessary to enable it to give judgment, request the Court of Justice to give a ruling thereon.

Where such a question is raised in a case pending before a court or tribunal of a Member State, from whose decisions there is no possibility of appeal under internal law, that court or tribunal shall be bound to bring the matter before the Court of Justice.

The article falls into two parts. First, a provision enabling any national court or tribunal (including administrative tribunals and special courts such as customs commissions or tax courts) to ask the European Court to give a preliminary ruling on any question of interpretation of the Treaty or of the validity and interpretation of measures taken by Council or Commission which is raised before the national court. Second, there is an obligation to make such a reference when the question is raised before a final court or tribunal, from whose decision there is no appeal. A considerable literature has grown up on the Court's jurisdiction under Article 177 and the way in which it is being used (or not being used) by national courts.[46]

There is no strictly corresponding provision in the E.C.S.C. Treaty. Article 41 of this treaty gives the Court sole jurisdiction to give preliminary rulings on the *validity* of 'conclusions' (i.e. decisions and recommendations) of the High Authority or the Council where their validity is in issue in proceedings before a national court. There is no express jurisdiction to rule on questions of interpretation of those acts of the High Authority or the Council.[47] Judge Donner has explained this difference between the treaties as deriving from the centralised character of the Coal and Steel Community, in which the treaty and other Community acts are applied directly by the High Authority and hardly at all through national laws or administrative acts. In contrast, the E.E.C. is a looser and more decentralised structure in which national courts and administrative authorities are regularly faced with questions of interpretation of the Treaty or Community legislation. Treaty questions arise frequently in cases involving the review of the legality of national administrative acts or legislation.

Consequently Article 177 provides for the probable frequency of such questions arising in national courts and makes reference to the European Court obligatory only for the highest court.[48]

Three brief observations about the Court's jurisdiction under Article 177 are appropriate before coming to consider a few of the ways in which questions of Treaty interpretation and Community law might be raised in our courts if the United Kingdom became a member of the Communities. First, although Article 177 seems to create an absolute obligation on the final courts to refer questions of Treaty interpretation or Community law to the European Court, the initiative rests with the national court.[49] There is no way in which the European Court can request, much less compel, a reference to itself. It is open to the national court to decide that no 'question' of interpretation arises because the Treaty provision or Community regulation is so clear as not to need interpretation. The French courts have shown a tendency to follow this path,[50] which may be understandable in the light of the French doctrine of *l'acte clair* but which can be dangerously simplistic when applied to Community legislation, which deals with complex economic and commercial subjects. Moreover, the six countries possess similar legal vocabularies, but with differing nuances of meaning.[51] However, a national court can quite properly decide that the Treaty question raised before it has already been the subject of a ruling by the European Court under Article 177 and that there is no need to refer the identical question again.[52]

The second observation is that the European Court has no power under Article 177 to pass judgment upon questions of the national law of member countries and has in fact been scrupulous to avoid references which seem to ask it to do this. Judge Mertens de Wilmars has written that the Court would have to reject a question from a national judge who asked whether such and such national legislation violated Community law. But it would accept the question if it sought to know whether the interpretation of Community law permitted the national judge to uphold a particular internal legal situation.[53]

Third, the object of Article 177 is to ensure uniformity of interpretation of Community law in the member States and to achieve this by co-operation between the European Court and national courts. A moment's reflection should reveal the vital importance to the development of the Communities of uniform interpretation and, consequently, application of Community law by the different national authorities. It is to be hoped that if the United Kingdom becomes a member all our judges—including chairmen of various tribunals, where appropriate, but in particular the judges of the appellate courts—will realise the implications of questions of Community law that may confront them and will be ready to co-operate with the European Court.[54] A company or individual, party to a case in a national court from which reference is made to the European Court, is entitled to plead in the proceedings before the European Court under Article 177.[55] But they cannot alter or add to the questions referred by the national court.

Concerning the ways in which questions of Community law could arise before British courts or tribunals very little can be said until the proposed legislation to give effect to the treaties and to the complex body of existing Community law has been published. But even under our present law there are provisions for challenging in the courts liability to customs duties, for example, or their amount, or liability to pay import levies on certain agricultural products. These could well be a model for provisions implementing comparable Community obligations.[56] For the future, Professor de Smith has expressed the view that British entry into the E.E.C. would 'powerfully reinforce the case for fundamental reforms in our own system of judicial review'.[57] Whether or not such reforms do follow upon British entry, it is certain that our membership would create an urgent and continuing need for education in Community law and its operation for our legal profession. It is of little use adhering to treaties which provide means of appeal to the European Court against alleged abuse of power or misinterpretation of law by Community organs if individuals and companies are unaware of these provisions and so unable to utilise them, and if our courts are also unaware of their essential role in applying and developing Community law in co-operation with the Court of Justice of the Communities.

NOTES

[1] Article 136 of the Euratom Treaty is identical. Article 31 of the E.C.S.C. Treaty adds 'and of the regulations made thereunder', but nothing turns on this. The Court has consistently regarded itself as the guardian of observance of Community law in all its forms. *Accord*, Valentine, *The Court of Justice of the European Communities*, Vol. 1, p. 274.

[2] 'Law and the European Community', *European Community,* supplement, 1967, p. 1.

[3] *Ibid.*

[4] Wall, *The Court of Justice of the European Communities,* London, 1966, p. 9.

[5] H.M.S.O., E.E.C. Treaty, 1967, p. 146.

[6] Articles 165–7, E.E.C.; Articles 137–9, Euratom.

[7] Article 167. Note that this translation, the Foreign Office revised unofficial translation of 1967, differs from the earlier Foreign Office version, which read: 'persons of indisputable independence who fulfil the conditions required for the holding of the highest judicial office in their respective countries or who are jurists of a recognised competence'. All the quotations in this chapter are from the revised 1967 translation. For a note on the virtues and defects of the several English versions of the treaties, none of which are official texts, see Valentine, *op. cit.,* Vol. 1, p. xv. An official English text will have to be agreed by all the member states if and when the United Kingdom and Ireland join the Communities. Cf. Chapter III.

[8] Cf. the composition of the E.E.C. Commission, Article 157(1).

[9] Article 165(4), E.E.C.

[10] Article 166(1), E.E.C.; Article 32(*a*), E.C.S.C.; Article 138, Euratom.

[11] Article 167, E.E.C.; Article 32(*b*), E.C.S.C.; Article 139, Euratom; Protocol on the Statute of the Court of Justice, Articles 2–7 (H.M.S.O., E.E.C. Treaty, 1967, p. 152).

[12] Article 166(2), E.E.C.

[13] Bebr, *Judicial Control of the European Communities,* London, 1962, p. 24; McMahon, 'The Court of the European Communities: judicial interpretation and international organization', 37 *B.Y.I.L.* (1961) 320, at p. 330; Pinto, *Les Organisations Européennes,* Paris, 1963, p. 268; Wall, *op cit.,* p. 190.

[14] 'Les Rapports entre la compétence de la Cour de Justice des Communautés Européennes et les tribunaux internes', 115 *Hague Recueil* (1965) 1, at p. 9.

[15] See Engelmann, *A History of Continental Civil Procedure,* London, 1928, trs. Millar, Book IV, 'Modern procedure', at p. 754.

[16] In the appeals for annulment, brought under Article 173, the Court is exercising an original jurisdiction and is not sitting on appeal from any national court. See p. 57 below.

[17] 'The Court of Justice of the European Communities', *I.C.L.Q.* Supplement Publication No. 1 (1961) 66, at p. 68.

[18] Principally Campbell, *Common Market law,* London, 1968, Vol. 1, Chapters 6 and 7; Wall, *op. cit.,* 1966, and Valentine, *op. cit.,* 1955 and (in two volumes) 1965. The Court makes its Rules of Procedure, which require the unanimous approval of the Council.

[19] Agreement was reached between the Law Society and the General Council of the Bar in May 1971, with the approval of the Lord Chancellor, that both barristers and solicitors should have the same rights as the *avocat* in the Protocol on the Statute of the Court. However, solicitors would be prohibited by an internal 'practice rule' from taking

part in oral presentation of cases referred under Article 177 (and like provisions in the E.C.S.C. and Euratom Treaties) from the Supreme Court or the House of Lords. Written presentation in such cases would have to be done in conjunction with a barrister. In other cases, solicitors would not be obliged to instruct a barrister and could conduct the whole case, both written and oral. But if they do instruct another *English* lawyer, it must be a barrister who is instructed. See *The Law Society's Gazette,* May 1971, pp. 193–4.

[20] 'Common law, statute law and Community law' in 'Law and the European Community', Supplement to *European Community,* 1967, p. 12.

[21] There are provisions for free legal aid: Rules of Procedure, Article 76.

[22] See p. 56 below.

[23] A party must pay for translation work done at his request which is considered by the Registrar to have been excessive: Rules of Procedure, Article 72(6).

[24] Articles 210, 211, E.E.C.; Article 6, E.C.S.C.; Articles 184, 185, Euratom.

[25] Protocol on the Statute of the Court, Article 37; Rules of Procedure, Article 93.

[26] The State is bound by the Treaty to take the measures required for enforcement of the Court's judgment: Article 171.

[27] Gilsdorf (of the Commission's Legal Service) in *European Community,* October 1970, p. 14.

[28] See Bebr, *op. cit., passim;* Valentine, *op. cit.,* Vol. 1, pp. 112–76; Campbell, *op. cit.,* Vol. 1, pp. 360–86.

[29] Article 174.

[30] Article 175.

[31] Article 176.

[32] Under the E.C.S.C. Treaty enterprises have more extensive rights of recourse to the Court.

[33] See Chapter VII, at p. 88, and Appendix 3.

[34] See *Milchwerke Heinz Wöhrmann & Sohn* v. *Commission* and *Alfons Lütticke G.m.b.H.* v. *Commission* [1963] C.M.L.R. 152.

[35] See note 5 above.

[36] Article 164, Euratom.

[37] Wall, *op. cit.,* p. 255. He draws attention to the language of the four official texts, which express the notion of title more clearly than the English version: 'forment titre exécutoire'; 'sind vollstreckbare Titel'; 'vormen executiorale titel'; 'costituiscono titolo escutivo'.

[38] Rules of Procedure, Article 71.

[39] E.E.C. Treaty.

[40] Article 171; see note 26 above.

[41] Article 88, E.C.S.C.

[42] Articles 174 and 176, E.E.C.; Articles 147 and 149, Euratom; Articles 34(1), 37(4) and 38, E.C.S.C.

[43] Articles 175 and 176, E.E C.

[44] Article 174, E.E.C.

[45] Note by President Lecourt in 15 *European Yearbook* (1967) 630 on 'The Court in 1967'; article by Lecerf in *European Community,* April 1971, p. 22.

[46] E.g. Judge Donner's Hague lectures, cited *supra,* n. 14; Michel Gaudet (Director General of the Legal Service of the Commission) 'The challenge of the changing institutions,' 3 *C.M.L.Rev.* (1965–6) 143, at p. 152; Mashaw, 'Ensuring the observance of law in the interpretation and application of the E.E.C. Treaty: the role and function of the *renvoi d'interprétation*', 7 *C.M.L.Rev.* (1969–70) 258 and 423.

[47] See submissions of Advocate General Lagrange in *Wagner* v. *Fohrmann* [1964] C.M.L.R. 245, at p. 250.

[48] *Loc. cit.,* p. 23. For discussion of the jurisdiction of national courts over questions of interpretation of the E.C.S.C. Treaty see Bebr, 'The relation of the E.C.S.C. law to the laws of the member States', 58 *Colum.L.Rev.* (1957) 767. See also Valentine, *op. cit.,* Vol. 1, pp. 233–4.

[49] And not with the parties to the litigation before the Court.

[50] *Re Shell-Berre* [1964] C.M.L.R. 462; *Re Riff* [1965] C.M.L.R. 29; *Etat Français* v. *Nicolas, ibid.* 36.

[51] Donner, *loc. cit.,* p. 45, and Chapter III of the present volume.

[52] *Da Costa en Schaake* v. *Netherlands Fiscal Administration* [1963] C.M.L.R. 224. See para. 28 of the U.K. *Legal and Constitutional* White Paper, Cmnd. 3301, and Mitchell in 5 *C.M.L.Rev.* (1967–8) 112, at p. 123.

[53] Mertens de Wilmars and Verougstraete, 'Proceedings against member States for failure to fulfil their obligations', 7 *C.M.L.Rev.* (1969–70), 385, at p. 388, n. 7.

[54] See Judge Donner's Hague lectures, *passim*; Gaudet in 3 *C.M.L.Rev.* (1964–5), 143, at p. 152; Mashaw in 7 *C.M.L.Rev.,* at p. 275 *et seq.* In replies to questions in the European Assembly the Commission has taken the view that a systematic refusal by a domestic court from which no appeal lay to refer questions under Article 177 *might* be considered as a failure of that member State within the meaning of Article 169.—*Journal Officiel,* 1967, No. 270/2, and *ibid.,* 1968, C.71/1 (replies to written questions No. 100/67 and No. 28/68).

[55] Statute of the Court, Article 20.

[56] Customs and Excise Act, 1952, s. 260(1)(b) and 260(2); Agriculture and Horticulture Act, 1964, s. 1, and Schedule, para. 1.

[57] *Judicial Review of Administrative Action,* second edition, London, 1968, p. 7.

[58] For enforcement of fines levied by the Commission, see p. 80 below.

[59] Cf. also ss. 1 and 2 of the Arbitration (International Investment Disputes) Act, 1966.

Chapter VI

MONOPOLIES UNDER THE E.E.C. TREATY

B. A. Wortley

I. FAIR COMPETITION THE BASIS OF THE E.E.C.

Competition is the method chosen to bring about prosperity in the Common Market countries. Article 2 of the E.E.C. Treaty defines one of the aims of the Community to be 'an accelerated raising of the standard of living . . .'

Competition, however, must be fair; there must be no assistance, overt or otherwise, by a member State to give its own nationals an unfair advantage over nationals of other member States.

Quantitative restrictions (quotas) on trade have virtually disappeared in the Common Market. The reduction and the ultimate disappearance of customs tariffs therein has been achieved in respect of industrial products in order to get rid of another obvious form of national protectionism. But there are other practices which may distort or prevent competition.

Any monopolist or near-monopolist can kill competition if he fixes prices which drive his competitors out of business and leave him in sole possession of a market, for the monopolist in sole control can raise prices to his own advantage, whatever the disadvantage to the consumer.

Monopolies were contrary to the policy of the common law (*Case of Monopolies*)[1] but, under the impact of nineteenth-century *laissez faire* liberalism, the common law was quietly weakened. Price-fixing by retail price maintenance agreements between supplier and retailer were in fact regularly enforced in the inter-war period. War-time rationing and price control may possibly have stirred public opinion to the dangers of monopolies, and the monopolies and restrictive practices legislation of more recent years has supplied English courts with tests to determine what are monopolies and also what price-fixing agreements are contrary to the public interest. The modern trend to render restrictive trade practices illegal is a general one in the free world. Professor

Friedmann, in his *Law in a Changing Society,* at p. 285, indicates 'the remarkable measure of agreement on this matter in the contemporary legislation of the U.S. and Canada and of the U.K., Germany, Norway, Sweden and the Netherlands'.[2]

To obtain a monopoly it is not, of course, necessary for there to be one single monopolist. It would be very difficult to remain a company large enough to monopolise the 200 million potential customers of the Common Market, and consequently an agreement which offends against British monopolies legislation might not be sufficiently restrictive to offend against the legislation designed to be applied throughout the whole Common Market.

The matter was put succinctly in the White Paper on the Common Market (February 1970): 'What would be the monopoly position within the U.K. would not necessarily remain one when the U.K. formed part of a larger market to which French and European companies have duty-free access.'[3]

Nevertheless, an agreement which does offend against the U.K. legislation on monopolies or on restrictive practices may continue to be attacked in our courts. If we join the Common Market and come under the jurisdiction of the Court of Justice of the E.E.C., then it may well be that such an agreement will also be subject to attack under the E.E.C. Treaty, just as our courts can hold that a contract is clearly contrary to the Restrictive Trade Practices Act, 1956, even before the Restrictive Practices Court so decides.[4]

It would indeed be difficult for one person or company to monopolise the whole Common Market. Of course, if, as Servan-Schreiber seems to suggest in *Le Défi américain,* in some fields superior American research and technology may enable American companies to dominate some types of European market, then the European Economic Community may have to take international action to protect its own interests. Meantime, the E.E.C. Treaty attempts to deal with monopolies and restrictive practices that arise inside the Common Market.[5]

II. RESTRICTIVE PRACTICES

The four heads of the rules on competition

The E.E.C. Treaty deals with the rules of competition under these heads:

1. Rules applying to undertakings, i.e. restrictive practices: Articles 85–90.

2. Dumping: Article 91.
3. Subsidies granted by States: Articles 92–94.
4. Fiscal provisions: Article 95.

In part III of this chapter and in Chapter VII we are chiefly concerned with restriction on competition, i.e. Articles 85–90,[6] but first, let us recall in this head that Article 91 enables protective measures to be taken during the transitional period by member States, guided by the Commission, to eliminate 'dumping practices' in inter-State trade.[7] The French, Italian, Dutch and German for 'dumping' is *dumping*! It remains to be seen what transitional period will be settled for the U.K. if she enters the E.E.C. The definition of dumping is contained in Article VI of G.A.T.T., where the cause or threat of injury to a domestic industry, rather than directly to the consumer, seems to be the test.[8]

Second, and also in passing, Articles 92–4 forbid State subsidies that distort competition in inter-State trade. Article 92(1) reads as follows:

> Except where otherwise provided for in this Treaty, any aid granted by a Member State or through State resources in any form whatsoever which distorts or threatens to distort competition by favouring certain undertakings or the production of certain goods shall, in so far as it adversely affects trade between Member States, be deemed to be incompatible with the Common Market.

According to *The Times* of 5 August 1971, in a despatch from Brussels of the previous day, the E.E.C. Commission, the body charged with seeing to the due execution of the Treaty, sent a communication to Italy stating

> that it must scrap the regional aids which it gives to the autonomous region of Friuli Venezia Giulia, which borders Austria and Yugoslavia and contains the port of Trieste. In a letter to the Italian government the commission claims that the aid which is given to this province is a disguised subsidy to industry there, which risks falsified competition within the Six and is therefore banned by Article 92 of the Rome Treaty. It has asked the Italian government to put forward its own views on its regional aid system for the area. If the Italians do not obey the commission's decision, the commission can take them to the European Court of Justice to force them to comply . . .

Article 92(2), which permits aid 'having a social character, granted to individual consumers', or 'to make good the damage caused by natural disasters', or to compensate certain regions of Germany for 'disadvantages' caused by the division of that country, is clearly not relevant here.

Italy's justification will need to be made by proving one of the special cases in Article 92(3). This reads as follows:

(*a*) aid intended to promote the economic development of regions where the standard of living is abnormally low or where there is serious under-employment;
(*b*) aid intended to promote the execution of an important project of common European interest or to remedy serious disturbance in the economy of a Member State;
(*c*) aid intended to facilitate the development of certain activities or of certain economic regions, provided that such aid does not adversely affect trading conditions to such an extent as would be contrary to the common interest. Any grants of aid to shipbuilding existing as on 1 January, 1957, shall, in so far as they serve only to offset the absence of customs protection, be progressively reduced under the same conditions as apply to the abolition of customs duties, subject to the provisions of this Treaty concerning common commercial policy in regard to third countries;
(*d*) such other types of aid as may be specified by the Council by qualified majority vote on a proposal of the Commission.

If Italy does not satisfy the Commission that the subsidy is justified under Article 92(3), then the Commission may require the aid to be abolished or modified within a specified period (Article 93(2)). Article 93 then permits the Commission or any other interested State to refer the matter to the Court of Justice of the Communities direct.

Normally, the decisions of the Court must be followed, even by States, as we have seen in Chapter V. However, a State not satisfied with the decision of the Court may yet approach the Council. Article 93(2)(iii) reads as follows:

The Council may, at the request of a Member State, unanimously decide that a grant of aid made or planned by that State shall be considered to be compatible with the Common Market, in derogation from the provisions of Article 92 or from the regulations provided for in Article 94, if such a decision is justified by exceptional circumstances. If the Commission has, as regards the grant of aid in question, already initiated the procedure provided for in the first sub-paragraph of this paragraph, the making of the request to the Council by the State concerned shall have the effect of suspending that procedure until the Council has made its attitude known.

If, however, the Council has not made its attitude known within three months of the said request being made, the Commission shall give its decision on the case.

Articles 93(3) and 94 provide for the making of regulations on exempted aid.

Campbell[9] suggests that any exceptional aid granted must not create a competitive advantage, and that it must be selective and enable the recipient to try to become self-sufficient. The E.E.C. Commission approved State aid to compensate German lead and zinc mines, in 1963, for losses caused by distortions on world markets.

McLachlan and Swann suggest that the E.E.C. Commission requires

First, an aid must never be permitted if it creates a competitive advantage. In other words, aids are allowed merely to offset disadvantages. Secondly, aids should be selective, that is they are granted to those who really need them rather than in a blanket fashion (a lesson learnt by the High Authority), and they should be temporary, decreasing in amount over time so as to compel the recipient to make increasing attempts to become self-sufficient.[10]

To prevent any further favouritism of the home trade by States, Article 95 provides:

No Member State shall impose, directly or indirectly, on the products of other Member States any internal taxation of such a nature as to afford indirect protection to other products.

A Member State shall . . . eliminate or amend any provisions existing . . . which conflict with the above.

In *Re Import Duties on Gingerbread: the Commission of E.E.C.* v. *the Grand Duchy of Luxembourg and the Kingdom of Belgium,*[11] the Court held that certain increases of duty imposed by the respondents, the Luxembourg and Belgian governments, after the coming into force of the E.E.C. Treaty, upon the granting of licences, *inter alia,* to import gingerbread, constituted charges 'having equivalent effect' to a customs duty, and the respondents were therefore in breach of the Treaty. The Court observed:[12]

The respondents have in effect claimed that this duty tended to 'equate the price of the foreign product and the price of the Belgian product'. They even doubted that it is 'compatible with the economy of the Treaty that in the heart of the Common Market producers of one country can acquire raw material at a better price than the producers of another member State'.

This argument ignores the principle according to which the activities of the Community include the establishment of a system guaranteeing that competition shall not be distorted within the Common Market (Article 3(*f*)).

To accept the argument of the respondents would lead, therefore, to an absurd situation which would almost be the exact opposite of the situation intended by the Treaty . . .

I have discussed elsewhere the seriousness with which distortion of competition is regarded in the E.E.C. Treaty (my *Jurisprudence*).[13]

Article 101[14] requires consultation between interested member States where a discrepancy between their laws or administrative provisions is interfering with competition, and, in the absence of agreement, provides for the issue of directives by the Commission. Article 102[15] attempts to provide that this process shall not be rendered null by future legislation distorting competition.

However, State security is safeguarded by Articles 223[16] and 224.[17] When security measures are alleged to result in unfair competition in the Common Market, Article 225[18] provides for a decision by the Court of Justice sitting *in camera*.

Article 226[19] deals with special difficulties in the transitional period.

So much for the rules affecting States. Individual *firms*, whether corporate or not, whether publicly owned or not,[20] are, however, mainly concerned to learn how they are affected by the rules on competition applicable directly to them, and the aim of the next section is to discuss the restrictive practices dealt with in Articles 85–90.

III. ARTICLE 86—DOMINANCE IMPOSED

Article 86 is perhaps the one to take first. It is aimed at the abuse or improper exploitation of a *dominant* position in the Common Market, i.e. a position which protects one from substantial competition.[21] This concept is well known in the separate laws of four of the six Common Market countries and in the Coal and Steel Treaty, Article 66.[22] Graupner rightly states[23] that an abuse cannot be the subject of exemption by the Commission. No 'fair law' can, by definition, countenance the abuse or improper use of power. Graupner does suggest, however, that minor instances of misuse might not be deemed to be caught by Article 86, and cites *Standard Oil Co. of New Jersey* v. *U.S.*[24] to the effect that insignificant restraints on competition producing minor effects are not to be regarded as violations. 'Price-fixing and market sharing', Graupner states, are illegal *per se*; patent agreements may not always be,[25] and the owner of a trade mark does not enjoy a dominant position 'merely because he can prohibit third parties from marketing products bearing the same mark in the territory of a member State' unless he can prevent effective competition in a considerable part of the market in question.[26]

In *Parke Davis & Co.* v. *Probel and Others*[27] it was made clear that a dominant position in the Market under Article 86 was not an infringement of the Treaty unless, for example, it also resulted in abusive exploitation.[28]

The full text of Article 86 is given as follows in the H.M.S.O. version of the Treaty:

Article 86

It shall be incompatible with the Common Market and prohibited, in so far as trade between Member States is liable to be affected by it, for one or more undertakings to exploit in an improper manner a dominant position within the Common Market or within a substantial part of it. Such improper practices may, in particular, consist in:

(*a*) the direct or indirect imposition of unfair purchase or selling prices or of other unfair trading conditions;
(*b*) the limitation of production, markets or technical development to the prejudice of consumers;
(*c*) applying in relation to like parties unequal conditions in respect of like transactions, placing them thereby at a competitive disadvantage;
(*d*) making the conclusion of contracts subject to agreement by the other parties to make additional payments, which, by their nature or according to commercial practice, have no connection with the subject of such contracts.[29]

The first paragraph makes it clear that there are general conditions to be fulfilled, (1) improper exploitation, (2) a dominant position, (3) capable of affecting a substantial amount of trade between member States and (4) in the Common Market. The various instances in (*a*) to (*d*) are examples of these general conditions not unlike those referred to in Article 85.[30]

Action against the dominant position of an enterprise is a matter which may be taken up in any part of the E.E.C. in respect of any enterprise, irrespective of its nationality and irrespective of the membership of its parent State in the Community. *Locus regit actum*. Those who do business on the Common Market have to accept its rules.

According to *The Times* of 19 March 1971, an important new move by the Commission has taken place:

The Common Market Commission decision to accuse the giant United States company Continental Can of having an 'unfairly dominant' position on the market in northern Europe marks a major new step in the E.E.C.'s policy of boosting competition within the Six. This is the first time in the 14 years of the Community's existence that *the Commission*[31] has ever tried to invoke Article 86 of the Rome Treaty . . .

This new move under Article 86 is not directed against a *de facto* monopoly as such, but is based upon an allegation of the violation of Article 86 which is aimed at abusive domination of a market.

In the words of the *Times* leader just quoted:

. . . the Commission is not accusing Continental Can of using its control of over 70 per cent of the market in Benelux and Germany—a control it obtained last year by buying up the market leaders there—to force up prices or to discriminate between customers. It is merely saying that the very act of buying up such a market share is an abuse of the Rome Treaty . . .

The remedy for any proved infringement of Article 86 may well be to order the enterprise to sell off part of its undertaking.

Although it is by no means certain that this power clearly exists, McLachlan and Swann say:

Thus the deterrent effect of the legal consequences that could follow from an offence under Article 86 may turn out to be quite considerable. It is, therefore, perhaps surprising to note that the other main anti-trust weapon that one would expect to be employed in this field, divestiture, has not in fact been specifically provided by the EEC. It may be that the absence of a specific provision for divestiture is inherent in the basic nature of Article 86 itself. By being solely concerned with the control of abuse and not, in contrast to the approach adopted in the ECSC and US, with the preservation of competition as such, Article 86 fails to opt for the market as the main technique of control. This could well lead to considerable indirect supervision or control of dominant enterprises by the Commission.[32]

This view is echoed by the *Times* leader just quoted:

The Commission is not just trying to find out whether its view of what constitutes an unfairly dominant position is held by the court. It is also trying to find out what, if anything, it can do if it proves its case. The Commission would almost certainly like to force Continental to sell off part of its empire. But the Treaty is a masterpiece of vagueness when it comes to spelling out the Commission's power in such cases: and the Council of Ministers has never passed regulations giving the Commission explicit rights in such matters.

From the words of Article 86, 'dans la mesure où le commerce entre Etats membres est susceptible d'en être affecté', 'so far as trade between member States is liable to be affectd by it' (H.M.S.O. translation) or 'may be affected thereby' (E.E.C. translation), the article may therefore be interpreted to refer to preventive action which can be taken by the Commission on its own volition (Article 89) to stop the implementation of offending practices; this resembles action which can be taken in the discretion of the English Chancery Court by injunction.

The examples of improper exploitation given in (*a*) to (*d*) of Article 86 seem to be examples and not necessarily restrictions on the general nature of paragraph 1.

Article 86 will certainly need to be considered when any mergers are contemplated to operate in the territory of the E.E.C. McLachlan and Swann have predicted:

> . . . in the longer run (and in the shorter run and even now in particular industries) a continuing merger movement could begin to throw up anti-trust problems. It is for this reason that we emphasize the need for a positive policy on mergers within the European Community. This should follow the example of the US, UK, and ECSC in so far as they provide means for nipping incipient market power in the bud. Thus some mergers may be dictated purely by the desire to exploit the consumer. Unfortunately, Article 86 is not well designed to deal with such a situation, since it only operates when a dominant position is being abused, whereas it would be desirable to prevent the power to abuse from emerging in the first place, provided that there were no compensating advantages from greater size. When it comes to mergers, Article 86 seems to lock the stable door after the horse has bolted.[33]

However, it seems that by friendly inquiries, or by more formal decision under Article 189, the Commission may often anticipate developments and prevent the horse from bolting.[34]

On the other hand, market sharing could occur when Company 1 kept its domestic market and Company 2, of a different nationality in the E.E.C., kept its domestic market. Article 86 would be relevant in this situation. McLachlan and Swann percipiently observe:

> . . . Thus the exploitation of its domestic market by each dominant enterprise could continue simply as a result of a consciously parallel course of action. It is this kind of apparently intractable situation that Article 86 can in fact deal with, as it is as much concerned with market domination by several enterprises as by one. For this reason alone, therefore, Article 86, in spite of its many appearances to the contrary, may yet turn out to be a potent weapon in the hands of the authorities . . .[35]

There is no procedure for the formal approval of mergers in the E.E.C. Treaty as there is in the treaty setting up the European Coal and Steel Community.[36] Advisers, therefore, will have to proceed on their own appreciation of the law. There is in Article 86 no procedure for 'clearance', as we shall see there is under Article 85 of the E.E.C. Treaty.

NOTES

[1] (1602) 11 Co. Rep. 846.

[2] A useful work on 'Comparative aspects of restrictive trade practices' was published by the *I.C.L.Q.* in its 1961 supplement.

[3] Cmnd. 4289.

[4] *Brekkes Ltd and another* v. *Cattel and others* [1971] 1 All E.R. 1031.

[5] For a full account, see *Droit des Communautés Européennes, les Novelles,* ed. Van der Meersch, Brussels 1969, pp. 795–867 (hereinafter 'Van der Meersch'), and for the literature on competition in the Common Market, pp. 805–10.

[6] See Campbell, *Common Market Law,* London, 1969, Vol. I, who deals with these in Chapter 3, pp. 156–280. (Hereinafter 'Campbell'.)

[7] S. 3 of the *Resale Prices Act,* 1964, is the comparable *internal* English law cited and discussed by Graupner, *The Rules of Competition in the European Economic Community,* The Hague, 1965, p. 51. (Hereinafter 'Graupner'.)

[8] For the literature, see Van der Meersch, p. 861. A valuable analysis of the policy of the E.E.C. Commission 1962–67 in relation to Article 85, by M. R. Mok, is to be found in 6 *C.M.L.Rev.* (1968) 67–103. For Article 85 before the domestic courts, see W. Alexander in 1 *C.M.L.Rev.* (1964) 431.

[9] *Op. cit.,* supplement (1970) to Vol. II, p. 51 (para. 2114).

[10] McLachlan and Swann, *Competition Policy in the European Community: the Rules in Theory and Practice,* London, 1967, p. 51. (Hereinafter 'McLachlan and Swann'.)

[11] Consolidated cases 2/62 and 3/62, [1963] C.M.L.R. 199. Followed in *Re Taxation of Imported Eaux de Vie, E.E.C. Commission* (case 16/69) [1970] C.M.L.R. 161.

[12] At p. 218.

[13] *Jurisprudence,* Manchester, 1967, pp. 210–13.

[14] *Article 101:*

'Where the Commission finds that a discrepancy between the provisions imposed by law, regulation and administrative action in Member States is interfering with competition within the common market and consequently producing distortion which needs to be eliminated, it shall consult the Member States concerned.

'If such consultation does not result in an agreement eliminating the distortion in question, the Council shall, on a proposal from the Commission, adopt the necessary directives for this purpose, unanimously during the first stage and thereafter by a qualified majority. The Commission and the Council may take any other appropriate measures provided for in this Treaty.'

[15] *Article 102:*

'1. Where there is reason to fear that the introduction or amendment of a provision imposed by law, regulation or administrative action may cause distortion within the meaning of Article 101, the Member State desiring to proceed therewith shall consult the Commission. After consulting the Member States the Commission shall recommend to the States concerned such measures as may be appropriate to avoid the distortion in question.

'2. If the State desiring to introduce or amend its own provisions does not comply with the recommendation made to it by the Commission, no request, in pursuance of Article 101, shall be made to other Member States to amend their own legislative or administrative provisions in order to eliminate such distortion. If the Member State which has ignored the Commission's recommendations causes distortion detrimental only to itself, the provisions of Article 101 shall not apply.'

[16] *Article 223:*

'1. The provisions of this Treaty shall not adversely affect the following rules:

(*a*) No Member State shall be obliged to supply information the disclosure of which it considers contrary to the essential interests of its security;

(*b*) Any Member State may take whatever measures it considers necessary for the protection of the essential interests of its security, and which are connected with the production of or trade in arms, munitions and war material; such measures shall, however, not adversely affect conditions of competition in the Common Market in the case of products which are not intended for specifically military purposes.

'2. During the first year after this Treaty comes into force, the Council shall, by a unanimous decision, determine the lists of products to which the provisions of paragraph 1(*b*) shall apply.

'3. The Council may, by a unanimous decision, on a proposal of the Commission, amend the said list.'

[17] *Article 224:*

'Member States shall consult one another with a view to taking in common the necessary steps to prevent the operation of the Common Market from being affected by measures which a Member State may be called upon to take in case of serious internal disturbances affecting law and order (*ordre public*), in case of war or serious international tension constituting a threat of war, or in order to carry out undertakings into which it has entered for the purpose of maintaining peace and international security.'

[18] *Article 225:*

'If measures taken in the circumstances envisaged in Articles 223 and 224 have the effect of distorting conditions of competition in the common market, the Commission shall, jointly with the State concerned, examine in what manner these measures can be adapted to the rules laid down by this Treaty.

'In derogation from the procedure provided for in Articles 169 and 170, the Commission or any Member State may bring the matter directly before the Court of Justice if it considers that another Member State is making an improper use of the powers provided for in Articles 223 and 224. The Court of Justice shall take its decision in camera.'

[19] *Article 226:*

'1. If, during the transitional period, difficulties arise which are serious and liable to persist in one section of the economy, or difficulties which could result in serious deterioration in a region's economic situation, a Member State may request authority to take protective measures in order to rectify the position and adapt the sector concerned to the economy of the common market.

'2. At the request of the State concerned, the Commission shall, by emergency procedure and without delay, determine the protective measures which it considers necessary, specifying the circumstances and the manner in which they are to be put into effect.

'3. The measures authorised under paragraph 2 may involve derogations from the rules of this Treaty, to such an extent and for such periods as are strictly necessary in order to achieve the objectives referred to in paragraph 1. Priority shall be given to the choice of such measures as will least disturb the operation of the Common Market.'

[20] See Schindler in 7 *C.M.L.Rev.* (1969–70) 57, at p. 58.

[21] Graupner, p. 27.

[22] Van der Meersch, p. 837.

[23] At p. 26.

[24] 221 U.S. 1 (1911).

[25] Van der Meersch, p. 835, para. 2080.

[26] *Sirena s.r.l.* v. *Eda s.r.l.* [1971] (European Court) C.M.L.R. 260.

[27] [1968] (European Court) C.M.L.R. 47.

[28] Akehurst in 43 *B.Y.I.L.* (1968–9), at p. 257.

[29] *Treaty establishing the European Economic Community, Rome, 25 March 1957,* London, 1967.

[30] See below, p. 79.

[31] Our italics.

[32] *Op. cit.,* pp. 226–7.

[33] *Op. cit.,* p. 456. See the Commission's communication on concentrations in the Common Market of 21 February 1966, No. 78.

[34] Van der Meersch, p. 848, paras. 2127 and 2128.

[35] *Op. cit.,* p. 225.

[36] 'Restrictive practices, etc., in the Common Market', *I.C.L.Q.* Supplementary Publication No. 4, 1962, p. 20.

Chapter VII

RESTRICTIVE PRACTICES UNDER THE E.E.C. TREATY

B. A. Wortley

1. ARTICLE 85—RESTRICTIONS IMPOSED

Unlike Article 86, Article 85 is not so much concerned with the more grandiose problems of 'dominance'. It is concerned with the effect on competition of price-fixing, the sharing of markets and restrictive trading practices, though even here matters can be of considerable moment. According to the *Times* leader of 19 March 1971, 'cartels in the dyestuff[1] and quinine industries were fined totals of $450,000 each'.[2] The power of the Commission to fine, as we shall see, is considerable, although not a criminal matter.

The second sanction of Article 85 is that arrangements which contravene it are 'null and void'. Since Regulation 17 came into force in March 1962, the Commission is the sole body to enforce and to exempt from the provisions of Article 85,[3] though of course the action of the Commission can be challenged in the Community Court.

Article 85 apparently somewhat draconically prohibits, on pain of automatically being 'null and void' (Article 85(2)), (*a*) agreements, (*b*) decisions, (*c*) concerted practices (i.e. it includes strictly contractual, as well as more informal arrangements) 'qui sont susceptibles d'affecter le commerce', 'which may affect trade'[4] between member States and 'the object or effect of which'[5] is to: (*a*) prevent, (*b*) restrict or (*c*) distort *competition* within the Common Market. Can any such agreement, decision or practice survive an attack on any of these grounds?

It is vital for the businessman to know what types of arrangement are objectionable under the Treaty[6] in the eyes of the Commission, before the Court of the Communities, or when invoked before a national court of a member of the E.E.C.

There are five principal objectionable arrangements:

1. Price-fixing agreements.
2. Limitations of production.

3. Market or supply sharing.
4. Customer discrimination.
5. Making the acceptance of contracts conditional on the assuming of some supplementary obligation.

Let us look at each head in turn.

Article 85(1)(a). Price-fixing

Agreements, decisions and concerted practices which amount to 'direct or indirect fixing of purchase or selling prices or of any other trading conditions' are prohibited by Article 85(1)(*a*).[7]

Let us look more closely at the decisions of the Commission in the *Quinine Case* and the *Dyestuffs Case*. Each has important lessons for us. To quote the report in the *Official Gazette of the European Communities*, No. L 193:

The first decision [of the Commission], adopted on 16 July 1969, concerns the 'international quinine agreement' to which all the major quinine producers in the Common Market belong. The six enterprises concerned hold a dominant position on the European market, and on the world market, in quinine. They are: a Dutch company (Nederlands Combinatie voor Chemische Industrie N.V. (Nedchem, of Amsterdam), two German companies (Boehringer Mannheim G.m.b.H. of Mannheim and Buchler and Co. of Brunswick), and three French companies (Société chimique Pointet–Girard S.A. of Villeneuve-la-Garenne, Société Nogentaise de Produits Chimiques of Nogent-sur-Marne and Pharmacie Centrale de France of La Plaine-Saint-Denis).[8]

Campbell[9] describes the facts and decision of the Commission in the *Quinine Case* as follows:

They agreed to charge common prices for quinine and quinidine in all countries. In 1964 they increased their selling price by about 50 per cent, despite some reluctance on the part of Nedchem. These single prices were applied by all six companies until February 1965.

The parties to the agreement agreed to protect their home markets —Germany, the Netherlands and particularly France—against imports from the other members.

The[y] established export quotas for all countries.

The French companies were not allowed to manufacture quinidine.

These agreements on prices, control of production and markets, and market-sharing are clearly illegal under Article 85 of the Treaty; indeed, the article quotes these as examples of agreements which are incompatible with the Common Market and prohibited.

The infringement was knowingly committed. The companies concerned obtained expert legal advice and were informed that their action constituted an infringement of Article 85 and that they were exposing themselves to Commission proceedings which might lead to their being fined. Despite this advice they continued their practices, filed no notification, and took what they believed to be adequate steps to keep the agreement secret. Amongst other things, they instructed all members to destroy compromising documents . . .

The Commission reacted strongly to the fact that there was failure to notify the agreement (and indeed, deliberate secrecy about it) so that there could be no occasion for exemption or for revision of it at the instance of the Commission.[10]

. . . the infringement is a serious one: it results from an accumulation of restrictions in the form of limitation of production, price-fixing, limitation of markets and market-sharing. Their gravity is accentuated by the fact that the enterprises in question control a large percentage of the market. Notwithstanding the undoubted difficulties encountered by the companies concerned in securing supplies of raw materials, the aims of the six manufacturers, and notably the fact that they collaborated in a selling price policy, are completely at variance with Article 85. There is the further point that this section of the chemical industry is concerned with public health and that there is no substitute for natural quinine in the treatment of certain types of malaria

The level of the fines has been differentiated in the light of the market position of each company and its degree of responsibility for the infringements. The fines were fixed at 210 000 u.a. for Nedchem, 190 000 u.a. for Boehringer, 65 000 u.a. for Buchler, 12 500 u.a. for Pointet–Girard, 12 500 u.a. for La Nogentaise and 10 000 for Pharmacie Centrale.

A unit of account is valued at 0·88867088 grammes of fine gold, or 10*p* (Protocol on Statute of European Investment Bank, Article 4). The smallest fine, for 10,000 u.a., was £1,000. The *Quinine Case* was upheld by the European Court of Justice on 15 July 1970.[11]

It is noteworthy that the action by the Commission in the *Quinine Case* was sparked off by the activities of the U.S. anti-trust authorities:

In mid-1966, after a spectacular increase in the selling price of quinine in the United States, the American antitrust authorities opened an investigation. Following the publication of their findings in 1967, the Commission began an inquiry into enterprises established in the Common Market and set an own-initiative procedure in train. It is this procedure which led to the adverse decision.[12]

The notion that resale price maintenance agreements are *prima facie* illegal is well known in U.S. law and is now part of English law (Resale Prices Act, 1964). But to offend against Article 85 the agreement must operate in the Common Market.

The *Dyestuffs Case* arose from the Commission's own inquiries:[13]

Acting on information supplied by trade organizations of industrial users in several EEC countries, the Commission carried out an investigation which showed that uniform and virtually simultaneous price increases had been applied in the Common Market by ten major manufacturers of dyestuffs in January 1964, January 1965 and October 1967. These manufacturers are Bayer, BASF, Cassella and Hoechst (Germany); Francolor (France); ACNA (Italy); Ciba, Geigy and Sandoz (Switzerland) and ICI (UK).[14]

Once again, no agreement had been registered and exemption could not be given under Article 85(3), nor was revision possible. The Commission held:

These concerted practices are caught by the provisions of Article 85(1). They restrict the free play of competition, which they confine to quality and technical assistance; by applying the same price increases for the same category of products on virtually the same date, they involve direct fixing of the selling prices of the dyestuffs marketed in the EEC by each of the manufacturers.

These practices can impair trade between Member States in two ways. Firstly, they cover all products imported and sold in the different EEC countries by the enterprises concerned and by their subsidiaries or representatives. Secondly, they prevent users from enjoying the benefits that could have accrued from importing from other Member States, since the price increases on their home market were applied at the same rate and on the same date in the other countries. It is the manufacturing companies rather than their subsidiaries which have been charged with concerted practices because the latter are closely dependent on their parent companies and did no more than obey instructions. The possible application of Article 85(3) could not be examined because no notification of an agreement had been filed. These are serious infringements by major companies controlling more than 80% of the EEC dyestuffs market. They must have known from their own competition experts that the concerted practices in question contravened the provisions of the Treaty.

This is the first time that the Commission has taken a formal decision on concerted practices in the matter of pricing and set out the criteria and reasoning which led it to conclude from the facts brought to light by its investigations that such concerted practices existed between the manufacturers concerned . . .

Given the gravity and the duration of the infringements, a fine of 50 000 u.a. is to be imposed on all the companies covered by the decision, the only exception being ACNA which has been less heavily penalized (40 000 u.a.) because it was not a party to the 1965 increase in Italy and, by its action, prevented the increase contemplated by the other manufacturers in 1967 being applied on the Italian market. By imposing these fines the Commission wanted to show its determination to implement an energetic policy of banning agreements contravening the rules of the Treaty, particularly in the case of major secret agreements, and thus to ensure observance of the Community's rules of competition.[15]

The Commission then went on to raise the extra-territorial effect of its decision, saying:

It is also the first time that a ban has extended beyond Community enterprises to companies with headquarters in non-member countries. These companies could be included in the scope of the decision because the restrictions of competition to which they were a party affected the situation within the Common Market.[16]

This point was taken up by the British Foreign Office in an *aide-mémoire* delivered to the Commission on 20 October 1969, in connection with the measures affecting I.C.I.[17] The *aide-mémoire* said:

In particular, the United Kingdom Government have for their part consistently objected to the assumption of extra-territorial jurisdiction in anti-trust matters by the courts or authorities of a foreign State when that jurisdiction is based upon what is termed the 'effects doctrine'—that is to say, the doctrine that territorial jurisdiction over conduct which has occurred wholly outside the territory of the State claiming jurisdiction may be justified because of the resulting economic 'effects' of such conduct within the territory of that State. This doctrine becomes even more open to objection when, on the basis of the alleged 'effects' within the State claiming jurisdiction of the conduct of foreign corporations abroad (that is to say, conduct pursued outside the territory of that State), such corporations are actually made subject to penal sanctions.[17]

This difficulty, which no doubt will also be raised in the Court of Justice of the Communities, where the *Dyestuffs Case* is now under consideration, will disappear in future cases from the United Kingdom if it accepts the Treaty of Rome.

The problem will still remain in respect of non-member States. Of course, even among members, not every restriction will be illegal.

In the case of *Grosfillex* (1964), a French company agreed that a Swiss company, Fillistorf, should have an exclusive agency for the distribution of plastic products at fixed prices *in Switzerland*. Clearly, this did not operate in Common Market territory and anything exported from Switzerland to that territory would be subject to customs duty. Moreover, there were other producers who could compete inside and outside that territory. The agreement was not objectionable.[18]

The contract concluded between the undertakings Grosfillex and Fillistorf has the aim of granting, by a manufacturer established within the Common Market to an undertaking established outside the Common Market, an exclusive concession of the sale of its articles for a territory situated outside the Common Market. The object of the contract is thus not to prevent, restrict or distort competition within the Common Market.[19]

However, in *Sirena s.r.l.* v. *Eda, s.r.l.*,[20] on a reference from the Civil and Criminal Court of Milan under Article 177, the European Court of Justice held that Article 85(1) on 'concerted practices' applies to

The simultaneous assignment to several concessionaires of national trade mark rights for the same product, if it has the effect of re-establishing rigid frontiers between member States, may prejudice trade between States and distort competition on the Common Market.[21]

As we have seen, the owner of a trade mark does not enjoy a dominant position under Article 86 merely as such.

Article 85(1)(b). Limitation of production

The limitation of production (e.g. by fixing quotas of production), of markets, of technical development or of investment, are all caught. They include 'vertical' marketing arrangements from producer to retailer and 'horizontal'[22] agreements between traders in the same goods.

Article 85(1)(c). Market or supply sharing

Market sharing or the sharing of sources of supply or services are also banned.

It is here perhaps that we might deal with the most important of all arrangements and one of the most difficult: the 'exclusive sales agency'.

The term 'agency' used here needs explanation. The ordinary agent (even a *del credere* agent) who acts for a principal, and who assumes no personal liability and does no more than make a contract to bind that principal, is not an 'agent' for the purposes of Article 85(1)(c).[23]

The 'agent' referred to is the independent trader who distributes goods for another, or who assumes a risk (other than a *del credere* one) in connection with his work. Where the 'agent's' object is to sell the products of a manufacturer—say, of motor cars—in part of the Common Market, the exclusivity of his agency may prevent an adequate supply. Normally this will not be what the manufacturer wants, and prudent manufacturers seeking good outlets will usually insist on a minimum amount of annual sales by the agent. But the manufacturer may himself be under a cartel arrangement to limit supplies and may have to limit or restrict operations in the market. In one case it has been indicated that

The extent to which exclusive sales concessions are affected by Common Market regulations depends on the terms of such concessions. If a manufacturer simply agrees not to sell his products to other dealers or consumers established in the area (e.g. Benelux) for which the exclusive sales concession has been granted, the municipal law governing the contract is unaffected by the Common Market regulations. The concession will, however, be contrary to the Common Market regulations if it is interpreted as obliging the manufacturer to prevent his customers established outside that area from re-selling within the area. (*Obiter*)[24]

This important point is made by Graupner:

In principle, Article 85 will only become operative if trade between Member States is affected by such an agreement. This means that an exclusive dealing agreement must have a direct effect on the inter-State trade of the E.E.C. It is therefore not sufficient that it affects only the market of one or more Member States (and might thus become subject to the national cartel law of such State (or States)). On the other hand, it is immaterial that the effect is brought about by an agreement between parties of whom one or even both are resident outside the Member States of the E.E.C. The application of the Rules of Competition of the Rome Treaty depends not on subjection of the parties concerned to the law of a Member State by virtue of territorial or personal jurisdiction, but solely on the test whether the inter-State trade between at least two Member States is affected. Whether administrative or judicial measures against any offending party can effectively be taken, and whether any such measure would be in conformity with public international law, is a different matter, which must be clearly distinguished from the question whether this inter-State trade is affected. Conversely, agreements between enterprises resident within two or more Member States or between one enterprise within and one outside a Member State which do not affect inter-state trade are outside Articles 85 and 86.[25]

Article 85(1)(d). Customer discrimination

This, according to the 1962 H.M.S.O. version, is 'the application of unequal conditions to parties undertaking equivalent engagements in commercial transactions, thereby placing them at a competitive disadvantage'.

The first part of the sentence is the translation by the United

Kingdom[26] of 'des conditions inégales à des prestations équivalentes' or 'condizioni dissimili per prestazioni equivalenti' or 'unterschiedlicher Bedingungen bei gleichwertigen Leistungen'. Dr Akehurst suggests that it would be better rendered as 'applying unlike terms to like transactions with other parties'. Personally, I prefer the translation by the E.E.C., 'unequal terms in respect of equivalent supplies', though instead of 'supplies' I would use the term 'contractual burdens'. The 1967 H.M.S.O. version reads: 'unequal conditions in respect of equivalent transactions'.

Whatever English text be adopted, the object of Article 85(1)(d) is to stop the unfair use of economic power to favour one set of customers rather than another.

Article 85(1)(e)

The imposition of supplementary obligations, i.e. 'making the conclusion of a contract subject to the acceptance by the other party to the contract of additional obligations which, by their nature or according to commercial practice, have no connection with the subject of such contract'. Examples of this might be the refusal to supply goods or services unless the person supplied undertook to buy other goods or other services.

II. EXEMPTIONS FROM ARTICLE 85 AND PROCEDURE THEREFOR

Article 85(3) does leave considerable room for manœuvre before condemnation under Article 85(1). It permits exemptions and it allows a *locus poenitentiae* by redrafting agreements which would otherwise contravene Article 85(1).

Article 85(3) provides two positive and two negative conditions that must be complied with if an agreement is not to offend against Article 85(1) and thus to be avoided, made *nul de plein droit* under Article 85(2).[27]

By Article 85(3), agreements, decisions or practices may be exempted:

First positive condition, if they contribute either 'to improve the production or distribution of goods *or* to promote technical and economic progress'. This is illustrated by the decision of the Commission in the *Netherlands Paint and Varnish Exporters*:

> ... the Commission considers that the only obligation which the agreement still imposes on the businesses in the group as far as their exports

to other EEC countries are concerned, namely the adherence to minimum quality requirements, does not in fact cause any appreciable restriction of competition. It has therefore been possible to give a negative clearance . . .[28]

Second, this is *on condition* that *positively* they allow 'consumers a fair share of the resulting benefit' (this is one of the objects of the Treaty). *Negatively,* they must not (*a*) 'impose on the undertakings concerned restrictions which are not indispensable to the achievement of the above objectives'; or (*b*) 'afford such undertakings the possibility of eliminating competition in respect of a substantial part of the products in question'.

Traders and others clearly need to know whether or not their marketing arrangements are exempt from invalidity or from any fine under the Treaty. Equally, the Common Market Commission has an interest to know of any limits on competition. Consequently, to enable a decision to be taken on the validity or otherwise of such arrangements and to bring possible infringements of Common Market rules into the open, a procedure of notification to the Commission has been set up.[29] This notification enables the Commission, or interested parties, or a member State, or a tribunal of such a State, or the competent authority of such a State to complain to the Commission that the agreements notified are contrary to the Treaty. Why then should anyone notify? There is no direct legal obligation to do so. In fact, those making the agreements are induced to notify because no fine for the infringement of Article 85(1) may be imposed so long as the Commission has not advised that the notified agreement contravenes Article 85(1).[30]

According to the 'Practical guide to Articles 85 and 86',[31] interested parties may request the Commission to say that there are no grounds for it to intervene under Article 85, with regard to an arrangement, decision or practice. This is called *a negative clearance.*

Notification is optional, then, but failure to notify and to get a negative clearance means that if the situation is misjudged by the parties, and Article 85 is infringed, there is no chance of exemption from invalidity and there is a possible fine.[32]

If a request for exemption under Article 85(3) is rejected, then the arrangement is prohibited retroactively from its inception or from 13 March 1962, if the agreement existed before that date.[33]

Again, as was made clear by the Commission in the *Quinine Case,* since the agreements there were deliberately kept secret and 'not notified to the Commission, there could be no question of their qualifying for exemption under Article 85(3)'.[34]

No fine will be imposed for the operation of an agreement in respect of the period after notification was due but before the request for negative clearance was rejected. Exemptions may be conditional and may need to be renewed. When exemption lapses or comes to an end, fines may be payable. Notification merely preserves conditional validity pending determination by the Commission of the applicability of Article 85(1).

It may well be that the case of *Consten-Grundig* v. *E.E.C. Commission*,[35] which held that the severance of an illegal agreement was possible, helped to satisfy the need to purge and to modify registrable agreements and to encourage 'consent decrees' so as to avoid penalties and to reduce the work of the Commission.

An example of a 'consented change' in a joint selling agreement for nitrogenous fertilisers, involving twenty-two Belgian and twenty-eight French manufacturers, is cited by Campbell, who says:

> The Commission found that they did in their original form infringe Article 85, partly because they hindered the expansion of exports of nitrogenous fertilisers within the Common Market. When notified of the 'provisions or arrangements challenged by the Commission', the participating firms declared their willingness to delete all clauses challenged. The Commission has thus been able to endorse the agreements in their amended form and to lift the ban on restrictive agreements for the period prior to the adoption of the Decision as well . . .[36]

One way of cutting down the administrative load has been for the Commission to grant *block exemptions* to save the need for notification and to save the Commission from being called upon to discuss the validity of many arrangements apparently notifiable under Article 85. Block exemptions from notification under Article 85 should certainly help the office of the Commission and cut down administrative costs. This again was, according to Campbell,[37] one result of the decisions of the Court of Justice of the Community in *Consten-Grundig* v. *E.E.C. Commission*[38] and *Italy* v. *E.E.C.* and *Technique Minière* v. *Maschin–bau Ulm*.[39] The Commission first proposed a draft *block exemption* from Article 85(1) in 1966, a revised draft in 1967 and, after consultation with interested parties, a final regulation was approved by the Committee of Experts and came into operation on 1 May 1967,[40] i.e. Regulation of the E.E.C. Commission 67/67/EEC of 22 March 1967[41] indeed now provides for block exemptions from notification in great detail.

I am informed by Mr R. Jaume, a director of Directorate (B) for Restrictive Agreements and Dominant Positions, in a letter dated 14 May 1971, that,

the Commission has received some 37,000 notifications, not 'since the E.E.C. was set up', as . . . stated in *The Times* of 19 March, but since 1962, when regulation n°. 17, the first implementing regulation pursuant to Articles 85 and 86 of the E.E.C. Treaty, was published. Some 7,000 of these notifications remained to be examined on 1 January 1971.

It should be said, however, that most—roughly 32,000—of the original notifications involved agreements between manufacturers in E.E.C. or third countries and their exclusive dealers in and/or outside the Common Market. Only a handful of these notifications have resulted in individual decisions. The bulk of them were dealt with through the Commission's communication on exclusive agencies of 24 December 1962, and more especially under the Commission's regulation n°. 67/67 of 22 March 1967, which granted a group exemption to exclusive dealerships without an export prohibition. Of these original 32,000 notifications of solus systems there still remain under consideration some 2,500 which are not covered by the aforesaid communication, regulation or test-case decisions.

It has been said that Article 85 is infringed when it actually diverts the 'natural flow' of goods between member States. As a result of the Commission's action, German toy manufacturers lifted bans on exports to parts of the Common Market.[42] The limitation of distribution to a particular agent may of course do this, but this alone cannot stop competition from other manufacturers in the E.E.C. The press release of 22 March 1967 quoted by Campbell states:

In the present state of trade, exclusive-dealing agreements in international trade improve the distribution of goods in general because the entrepreneur can concentrate his sales operations, can avoid maintaining business with only one dealer, and can more easily overcome any difficulties which stem from linguistic, legal or other differences. Appointing an exclusive dealer makes it easier to promote the sale of a product and leads to intensive marketing and a steady flow of goods coupled with more rational distribution. In addition, the appointment of a single dealer or exclusive purchaser who, on behalf of the manufacturer, meets expenditure for sales promotion, after-sales service and stocking offers an opportunity to many small and medium-size enterprises to compete on a market which would otherwise be beyond their reach. The parties to a contract must remain free to decide whether and how far they will accept undertakings to promote sales in their agreements. Improvements in distribution arise, however, only if no competitor is entrusted with sales of the product.

As a rule such exclusive-dealing agreements also confer on consumers an equitable share in the resultant benefit, as they draw direct advantage from more efficient distribution and their economic or supply situation is improved inasmuch as they can obtain products manufactured abroad more swiftly and more conveniently.

In addition to the exclusive-dealing clause, the following restraints on competition will be allowed in contracts qualifying for block exemption:

1. An undertaking neither to manufacture nor offer for sale goods competing with the goods covered by the contract, during the life of the contract or up to one year after it lapses (ban on sale of competing products).
2. An undertaking not to prospect for customers in respect of the products covered by the contract, not to set up establishments and not to maintain stock points outside the area covered by the contract (ban on prospecting for customers).[43]

It has been decided on a reference from the Munich Court of Appeal that an exclusive agency escapes ban under Article 85(1) if the parties are weak in the market for the products concerned.[44]

Exclusive dealing agreements between two parties only

These need no notification to the Commission until 31 December 1972. After then the position will no doubt be reviewed in the light of experience.

I am further informed by Mr Jaume that in addition to exclusive dealing agreements,

a second important group of notifications—about 3,600 of them—involve licensing agreements. Some of them have meanwhile been terminated. The remaining 3,300 are presently under consideration. Test cases will be selected for individual decisions which, by analogy, will be applicable to a number of licensing agreements notified to the Commission.

The remainder—about 1,400 notifications, of which 200 are still to be dealt with—mostly involve horizontal agreements of various sorts. A number of these agreements, in so far as they included restrictive provisions and/or practices prohibited under the competition rules of the E.E.C. Treaty, have been voluntarily abandoned or amended by the parties concerned after discussion with the Commission's services, sometimes after a formal communication concerning the points of objection; the relevant notifications were then filed without any further decision. Others were covered by the Commission's memorandum on inter-enterprise co-operation of 29 July 1968. A small number resulted in individual decisions, either favourable (granting a negative clearance or the benefit of Article 85(3) of the E.E.C. Treaty) or disapproving, as in the cases of the quinine and dyestuffs cartels.

The administrative load is enormous and much ingenuity has indeed been expended to relieve the burden.

III. CONSIDERATIONS APPLICABLE TO BOTH ARTICLES 85 AND 86

Finally, a few points which relate to both Articles 85 and 86.

1. From Article 90 it seems that these rules also apply to 'public undertakings'.[45]

2. Article 88 leaves it to the competent authorities in member States to enforce Articles 85 and 86 pending regulations and directives binding on members. Indeed, Articles 87 and 88 'provide the *machinery to operate* Articles 85 and 86'.[46] Article 89 confirms the jurisdiction of the Commission. The Commission can act on its own initiative, and for this purpose it may act on the evidence of foreign investigations: the inquiries made in the *Quinine case* have already been referred to.[47]

3. Articles 85 and 86 both apply to 'enterprises', i.e. to enterprises or undertakings or groups of persons or companies or partnerships with an economic life of their own. The realist theory of legal personality dominates here and, as Gower[48] has said, is being more and more recognised in company law.

McLachlan and Swann say:

> It is important to note that the anti-trust rules refer to enterprises, and whatever their legal form—whether it be corporate body, partnership, or independent trader—they are included. The concept of an enterprise does, however, give rise to some legal difficulty. It would be unreasonable to expect a wholly-owned subsidiary to compete with the parent company and in this case common sense would treat the two as one enterprise. But the possibility exists that one company may have a limited participation of, say, 5 or 10 per cent in another. Such a participation would not unify the enterprises but clearly, at some higher level of participation, the situation would change and the two enterprises would in effect become one, and agreements between them could not be brought within the ambit of the anti-trust rules. Until cases actually arise it is impossible to say where this line is going to be drawn . . . Article 90 requires that public undertakings and undertakings to which member States grant exclusive rights (nationalized industries are clearly covered by these two categories) shall not engage in practices contrary to Article 85. The same article also states that concerns entrusted with the management of services of a general economic interest or having

the character of a fiscal monopoly shall be subject to the anti-trust rules 'in so far as the application of such rules does not obstruct the *de jure* or *de facto* fulfilment of the specific tasks entrusted to such concerns'.[49]

Campbell points out that:

In *Re Christiani and Nielsen NV* [1969] CMLR D36 the Commission held that where a subsidiary is wholly owned by its parent company, and it is found as a matter of fact that the subsidiary is not able to engage in economic action which is autonomous of its parent company, then in spite of their separate legal entities the two companies will be regarded as one for the purposes of Community competition law . . .[50]

4. Fines imposed for breach of Articles 85(1) or 86 are not penal but do require the element of deliberation or of negligence.[51]

5. There is no procedure for specific performance as we know it, but the French system of *astreintes* may be used to compel acceptance of the decisions of the Commission. This consists in penalising the offender for every day he fails to obey the decision.[52]

Article 85 perhaps presents the most important problems for businessmen operating in the Common Market. Its operation is ensured by the Commission, but the legality of an act of the Commission may be challenged in the Community's Court of Justice at Luxembourg.[53]

We cannot do better than conclude this chapter with the words of James Fawcett:

The prohibition of unfair competition can be regarded as a general principle of law to be found in the municipal law of many countries; it has also had international recognition in the 'open door' system of the General Act of Berlin, 1885, [on Africa] and in the mandates and trusteeship agreements, and has now been embodied in the E.E.C. Treaty as a central feature.[54]

Upon the success of the Commission's efforts will depend the future of the consumer in the vast Common Market.

NOTES

[1] See *aide-mémoire* of the United Kingdom government, 20 October 1969, on the Dyestuffs Case and I.C.I., reprinted in *B.P.I.L.*, 1967, p. 58.

[2] Campbell, *op. cit.*, 1970 supplement, p. 49.

[3] See Thompson in 13 *I.C.L.Q.* (1964), at p. 845. See Appendix 3.

[4] This is the 1967 revised version of H.M.S.O. Professor Cohn, in 13 *I.C.L.Q.* (1964), at p. 1469, had said with regard to the 1962 H.M.S.O. version reading 'which are liable to affect trade':

'The EEC version as well as the Stationery Office version fail to convey the strictness of all four official versions. It is not at all necessary that there should be a likelihood that inter-State trade should be affected, or that it should be liable that this should happen. The mere possibility of its happening is enough, according to the Dutch and Italian versions. The French and German versions merely add to this that the possibility must be flowing from the nature of the agreements, decisions and concerted practices.

'It is submitted that the agreements, decisions and concerted practices to which Article 85 refers, are those which are "capable of affecting trade". In this sense it has been understood by Professor Stefan A. Riesenfeld in his essay on "Protection of competition" in *American Enterprise in the European Common Market,* Vol. 2 (Ann Arbor, 1960, p. 327). The phrase "capable of" is the correct rendering of the French "susceptible" and is compatible with the Dutch and Italian versions.'

[5] The expression 'are designed' was the expression used in the unofficial text of H.M.S.O. (1962) in relation to these forbidden attacks on free competition, as the translation by H.M. government of the French text, 'qui ont pour objet ou pour effet', the Italian 'che abbiano per oggetto o per effeto' and the German 'geeignet sind'. The English unofficial translation by the Community, 'have as their object or result', seems preferable, and is accepted in the 1967 H.M.S.O. version.

[6] For certain limitations on the retroactivity of the annulling and avoiding of these arrangements, see Van der Meersch, p. 841, para. 2102.

[7] For certain types of agriculture, Article 42 limits the rules of competition until the Council has accepted the proposals of the Commission.

[8] The Commission's decision is also reported in [1969] C.M.L.R. (Restrictive Practices supplement), D 41.

[9] Supplement to Vol. I, p. 48, para. 3.18.

[10] *Official Gazette of the European Communities,* No. L 193 of 5 August 1969, p. 30.

[11] *A.C.F. Chemieforme N.V.* v. *E.E.C. Commission,* Case 41/69, *Recueil de la jurisprudence,* 1970, p. 661; *Buchler & Co.* v. *E.E.C. Commission,* Case 44/69, *ibid.,* p. 733; *Boehringer Mannheim G.m.b.H.* v. *E.E.C. Commission,* Case 45/69, *ibid.,* p. 769; [1971] C.M.L.R. The three judgments are summarised in 8 *C.M.L.Rev.* (1971) 86.

[12] Official report of the E.E.C. Commission 9/10, 1969, p. 30.

[13] *Ibid.,* p. 31.

[14] *Official Gazette of the European Communities,* No. L 195 of 7 August 1969, p. 31.

[15] *Ibid.*

[16] *Ibid.*

[17] See *B.P.I.L., 1967,* p. 58.

[18] 'L'article 85, par. 1er, énumère un certain nombre d'accords susceptibles d'avoir des effets anticoncurrentiels . . . Y figurent les accords ou pratiques qui consistent à: ". . . Appliquer à l'égard de partenaires commerciaux des conditions inégales à des prestations équivalentes en leur infligeant de ce fait un désavantage dans la concurrence." Ce texte, contrairement aux articles 4(*b*) et 60 du traité C.E.C.A., ne saurait être

considéré comme contenant une interdiction générale de toutes les discriminations . . .' (Van der Meersch, p. 823, para. 2037). Negative clearance has been given for an exclusive dealing agreement in Japan, outside the Common Market (Campbell, 1970 supplement, p. 51, para. 3.19).

[19] Decision of the Commission of the European Economic Community (64/233/E.E.C.). 11 March 1964; [1964] C.M.L.R. 237, p. 238.

[20] [1971] C.M.L.R. 260.

[21] At p. 274.

[22] See Cairncross, *Introduction to Economics,* second edition, London, 1955, p. 165. See Van der Meersch, p. 820, where it is suggested that Article 85(1)(*a*) and (*c*) aims at vertical arrangements.

[23] For the German law on sole distribution see Cohn, *Manual of German Law,* London, 1971, Vol. II, p. 24.

[24] *Bara* v. *Advance Transformer Co., Philips (Netherlands) and Philips (Belgium),* before the Tribunal de Commerce de Bruxelles, [1964] C.M.L.R., at p. 379.

[25] *Op. cit.,* p. 127.

[26] H.M.S.O., London, 1962, p. 32.

[27] See Akehurst above, Chapter III, pp. 25–6.

[28] Campbell, 1970 supplement, p. 57.

[29] Campbell, Vol. I, p. 271.

[30] Campbell, Vol. I, p. 263.

[31] Campbell, Vol. II, p. 255, at p. 259.

[32] Van der Meersch says:

'En ce qui concerne la situation juridique des ententes avant la décision de la Commission sur l'application éventuelle de l'article 85, par. 3, trois thèses ont été proposées.

'D'après le première, l'entente est "provisoirement non valable", cette situation s'appartenant à celle que le droit allemand connaît sous le nom de "schwebende Unwirksamkeit" . . .

'D'après la seconde, la question doit rester ouverte et le juge éventuellement saisi doit surseoir à statuer tant que la Commission n'a pas pris de décision . . .

'D'après la troisième enfin, l'entente est "provisoirement valable".' (*Op. cit.,* pp. 833–4, para. 2073.)

He concludes:

'La situation juridique des ententes entre le moment de la notification ou la naissance de l'entente (pour celles dispensées de cette formalité) et la décision de la Commission est en fait une situation hybride: elles ne sont pas définitivement nulles, puisqu'elles peuvent être rétroactivement reconnues valables; elles ne sont pas non plus pleinement valables, puisqu'en cas de refus de la Commission d'octroyer le bénéfice de l'article 85, par. 3, le nullité rétroagit jusqu'au jour de la notification . . .' (P. 834, para. 2075.)

[33] The date on which Regulation No. 17 of the Council of the E.E.C., the First Implementing Regulation pursuant to Articles 85 and 86, came into force. See the E.E.C. *Manual for Firms,* 1962, p. 3.

[34] See above, p. 86.

[35] [1966] C.M.L.R. 418, European Court; see the form of the Decision, p. 481.

[36] 1970 supplement, p. 53.

[37] Campbell, Vol. I, p. 206.

[38] [1966] C.M.L.R. 418.

[39] *Ibid.*, 357.

[40] J. O. (894) 67: [1967] C.M.L.R. D1.

[41] Campbell, Vol. I, p. 210.

[42] Campbell, 1970 supplement, p. 53.

[43] Campbell, Vol. I, p. 210.

[44] Judgment 5/69 of 9 July 1969: *Franz Völk v. Ets. Vervaeke,* S.p.r.l. [1969] C.M.L.R., 273.

[45] Van der Meersch, p. 800, paras. 1987 and 2172 *et seq.*

[46] Campbell, Vol. I, at p. 223. For the position since Regulation No. 17 came into effect, see above, p. 79.

[47] Above, p. 80.

[48] *Modern Company Law,* third edition, London, 1969, p. 216.

[49] *Op. cit.*, p. 130.

[50] 1970 supplement, p. 52.

[51] Van der Meersch, p. 842, para. 2105.

[52] *Ibid.*, p. 842, paras. 2108 and 2109.

[53] *S.A. Cimenteries C.B.R. Cementsbedrijven N.V. and others* v. *E.E.C. Commission, Recueil de la jurisprudence,* Vol. 13, 1967, p. 93; [1967] C.M.L.R. 77.

[54] 40 *B.Y.I.L.* (1964), at p. 57.

Appendix I

LEGAL AND CONSTITUTIONAL IMPLICATIONS OF UNITED KINGDOM MEMBERSHIP OF THE EUROPEAN COMMUNITIES[*]

PRELIMINARY

1. The purpose of this paper is to assess the implications for the laws and the legal systems of this country and for the legislative functions of Parliament if we became a member of the European Communities. The assessment is based on a study of the terms of the three European Treaties, their subordinate instruments, and other Community documents. The paper is concerned with the general legal questions that would arise for the United Kingdom and does not attempt to give an account of the provisions governing the various economic, social and commercial matters dealt with by the Treaties. Any study of those provisions would have to take account of numerous exceptions relating to individual Member States which are contained in the Treaties and their subordinate instruments, and also of derogations by individual Member States from the strict application of various obligations which have taken place in practice. These exceptions and derogations indicate that the principles of the Treaties are applied pragmatically, and that allowances are made for the particular circumstances of Member States.

2. The Treaties contain provisions of two kinds. Some provisions describe the objectives which are agreed upon between the Member States, leaving it to them to achieve those objectives by legislative or administrative action—a method followed, for example, in the field of customs duties. Other provisions are intended to take effect directly as law in each of the Member States, e.g. the provisions relating to restrictive practices.

3. Treaty provisions of the former kind have hitherto been more usual, but provisions resembling the latter kind are by no means unknown to the law of the United Kingdom. They occur, for example, in various Conventions relating to carriage by air or by sea and to the regulation of sea fisheries, and are embodied in our domestic law by a series of Acts passed for the purpose.

4. The novel features of the European Treaties lie first in the powers conferred on the Community institutions to issue subordinate instruments which themselves may impose obligations on the Member States or may take effect directly as law within them; and secondly in the powers of those institutions to administer and enforce (subject to the control of the European Court) much of the law deriving from the Treaties and the instruments made under them.

THE COMMUNITY INSTITUTIONS AND THEIR FUNCTIONS

5. The Community institutions consist of the following:

(*a*) A single Assembly, now known as the European Parliament, which exercises functions under all three Treaties. It has 142 Members at present nominated by the Parliaments of the Member States from among their members (EEC Treaty, Articles 137 to 144, EURATOM Treaty, Articles 107 to 114, ECSC Treaty, Articles 20 to 25).

(*b*) A separate Council of Ministers under each Treaty, consisting of one representative of each Government of the Member States[1] (EEC Treaty, Articles 145 to 154, EURATOM Treaty, Articles 115 to 123, ECSC Treaty, Articles 26 to 30).

(*c*) A separate body known as the Commission in the EEC and EURATOM Treaties and as the High Authority in the ECSC Treaty. The EEC Commission consists of nine members, of which not more than two are of the same nationality. The EURATOM Commission consists of five members, each of a different nationality. The High Authority consists of nine members, of which not more than two are of the same nationality. Each of the Treaties provides that this body is to carry out its functions in complete independence and in the general interests of the Community (EEC Treaty, Articles 155 to 163, EURATOM Treaty, Articles 124 to 135, ECSC Treaty, Articles 8 to 19).

(*d*) A single Court of Justice, consisting of seven judges and two Advocates General, exercising jurisdiction under each of the three Treaties (EEC Treaty, Articles 164 to 188, EURATOM Treaty, Articles 136 to 160, ECSC Treaty, Articles 31 to 45).

(*e*) A number of ancillary bodies mostly of a consultative nature.

6. Under a Treaty signed on 8th April 1965 (known as the Treaty of Fusion), the three Councils are to be amalgamated into a single new body to be known as the Council of the European Communities (Article 1), and the two Commissions and the High Authority are to be amalgamated into a single new body to be known as the Commission of the European Communities (Article 9). It was envisaged that this Treaty would enter into force on 1st January 1966, but it has not yet been ratified by all Member States.[2]

7. *The European Parliament* is a deliberative and consultative body having (except in one matter) no legislative or executive functions.[3] Its influence is exercised through public opinion expressed in open debate. It must have an annual session and in practice meets more frequently at the request of a majority of its members or at the request of the Council or the Commission or High Authority. The European Parliament has the ultimate sanction of a vote of censure on the activities of the Commission and the High Authority which, if carried by a two-thirds majority of the votes cast representing a majority of the members, operates to require the resignation *en bloc* of the censured body. Such a censure vote may be moved at any time against the Commission but,

in the case of the High Authority, can be moved only on the presentation of the report which the High Authority (like the Commission) is required to present annually to the European Parliament. In addition, the European Parliament is required to be consulted before the exercise of many of the Council's more important powers to issue subordinate instruments under the EEC Treaty, and a few of the powers of the Council under the EURATOM Treaty. It is also entitled to consider and propose amendments to the budget.

8. *The Council of Ministers* is, in each case, the body which controls the overall direction of the Community, though its powers under the EEC and EURATOM Treaties are more extensive than under the ECSC Treaty.

9. *The Commission and the High Authority* are the executive bodies of the Communities, responsible for their day-to-day management and exercising enforcement powers.

10. *The Council of Ministers and Commission* under the EEC and EURATOM Treaties and the *High Authority* under ECSC Treaty are the bodies by whom the powers of issuing subordinate instruments are exercisable: see Article 189 of the EEC Treaty, Article 161 of the EURATOM Treaty and Article 14 of the ECSC Treaty. The two first-mentioned Articles are in identical terms. Their first paragraph provides that 'In order to carry out their task and in accordance with the provisions of this Treaty, the Council and the Commission shall make regulations and issue directives, take decisions, make recommendations or give opinions'. The main instrument having direct internal effect is the regulation. This is stated to 'apply generally', to 'be binding in its entirety' and to 'take direct effect in each Member State'. A decision may also have direct internal effect. It is stated to 'be binding in its entirety upon those to whom it is directed'. Decisions are appropriate for imposing obligations or liabilities upon, or granting rights or exemptions to, particular undertakings or individuals. They may also be directed to Member States; in that case they are used more in the sphere of administration than of legislation.

11. A directive imposes obligations only on Member States. It is described as 'binding, as to the result achieved, upon each Member State to which it is directed, while leaving to national authorities the choice of form and methods'.

12. Recommendations and opinions are stated to 'have no binding force'.

13. Some of these terms have different meanings when used in the ECSC Treaty. Article 14 enables the High Authority 'to take decisions, make recommendations and give opinions'. Decisions are stated to 'be binding in their entirety'. They are of the executive type, although they often apply to classes of undertakings, and are the means by which the High Authority exercises its powers of regulation and control over the two industries affected by the Treaty. Recommendations are described in much the same terms as directives in the other two Treaties. They are to be binding as to objectives but with choice as to means, and are used to impose obligations on Member States and undertakings.

Opinions are stated not to be binding, and have the same status as recommendations and opinions under the other two Treaties.[4]

14. The Treaties regulate the manner in which the Council of Ministers is to reach its decisions. The voting rule in the EEC is that the Council's resolutions are reached by a majority of its members, except where otherwise provided in the Treaty. However, nearly all the powers of the EEC Council to enact regulations or to issue directives are exercised unanimously or by what is known as a 'qualified majority', that is a majority of 12 votes out of 17.[5] The completion of the second stage of the Community's transitional period and the commencement of the third stage on 1st January 1966, carried with it the consequence that, while a substantial number of important matters would continue to be decided by unanimity, certain matters previously to be decided unanimously (e.g., commercial relations with third countries under Article 111.3) were henceforward to be decided by qualified majority vote. This change in voting procedure was, however, accompanied by differences of opinion among the Six. At their meeting at Luxembourg in January 1966, they agreed that when, in the case of decisions which may be taken by majority vote on a proposal of the Commission, very important interests of one or more Member States were in question, members of the Council are to endeavour to reach within a reasonable period solutions which could be adopted unanimously. The French delegation considered that when very important interests were in issue discussion should continue until unanimous agreement was reached; but this was not accepted by the other countries, and it was simply noted that there was a difference of opinion within the Six on what happened when a complete resolution of the divergent views was not achieved. In the case of the EURATOM Treaty the requirement of unanimity or a qualified majority applies to many of the more important powers of the Council.

15. In exercising its powers to make instruments the Council acts in most instances on a proposal by the Commission and in such cases, even in matters where the Council is empowered to act by less than a unanimous vote, it may only amend the Commission's proposal unanimously. As already stated consultation with the European Parliament is required in many of the more important instances, and the two Treaties also make provision in appropriate cases for consultation with the Economic and Social Committee.

16. The position under the ECSC Treaty is different, because under Article 14 the High Authority is the principal instrument-making body and the role of the Council is largely consultative and approbatory.[6] Broadly speaking the Treaty requires the Council to be consulted before the exercise of important powers, and in many cases the High Authority's proposal has to receive the approval of the special majority laid down by Article 28.3 of the Treaty[7] and in some cases the unanimous approval of the Council. There are also comprehensive requirements for consultation with the Consultative Committee.

17. The procedures regulating the exercise of the powers of the institutions of the Communities are accordingly designed to ensure full

discussion with Member States and, where appropriate, a thorough examination of technical aspects before binding decisions are taken.

18. *The European Court of Justice* is a single court exercising jurisdiction conferred under each of the three Treaties. The seven judges and the two Advocates General are required to be chosen from persons whose independence is beyond question and who are qualified for the exercise of the highest judicial office in their respective countries or who are otherwise lawyers of the highest standing. It can be assumed that in the event of the United Kingdom becoming a member of the European Communities the Court would include a member from the United Kingdom. The jurisdiction of the Court falls into three main categories:

(*i*) Jurisdiction in proceedings brought against a Member State by the Commission or another Member State for a breach of its obligations under the EEC or EURATOM Treaties (see Articles 169 to 171 or the EEC Treaty and 141 to 143 of the EURATOM Treaty; there are no corresponding provisions in the ECSC Treaty). This jurisdiction is the normal one for an international court. The Court's judgment establishes the breach, but does not impose legal sanctions against the offending State. Defaulting States are relied upon to remedy any breach of their obligations found by the Court.

(*ii*) Supervision of the exercise of the powers of the Community institutions, not only in proceedings brought by Member States or by other Community institutions but also in proceedings brought by undertakings or individuals challenging the validity of acts of the institutions, appealing against penalties or claiming damages.[8] (See Articles 172 to 176 and 178 of the EEC Treaty, 144, 146 to 149 and 151 of the EURATOM Treaty, and 33 to 38 and 40 of the ECSC Treaty.)

(*iii*) Jurisdiction to rule on questions arising in national courts and tribunals on the interpretation of the provisions of the EEC or EURATOM Treaties and the regulations and other instruments made under them. The great majority of cases brought before the Court under the EEC Treaty fall under this category. There is also jurisdiction under all three Treaties to rule on questions arising in national courts and tribunals on the validity of the instruments made under them. National courts are enabled, and in the case of courts from which there is no appeal are required,[9] to refer such questions to the European Court (see Article 177 of the EEC Treaty, 150 of the EURATOM Treaty and 41 of the ECSC Treaty).

19. Judgments of the European Court and decisions of the Council, Commission or High Authority imposing sanctions on individuals and undertakings are to be enforced by national courts (see Articles 187 and 192 of the EEC Treaty, Articles 44 and 92 of the ECSC Treaty, and Articles 159 and 164 of the EURATOM Treaty).

COMMUNITY LAW

Application by the United Kingdom Parliament

20. If this country became a member of the European Communities it would be accepting Community law. By 'Community law' is meant the whole body of legal rights and obligations deriving from the Treaties or their instruments, whether conferred or imposed on the Member States, on individuals or undertakings, or on the Community institutions. A substantial body of legislation would be required to enable us to accept the law.

21. In the first place provision would have to be made for those matters on which the Treaties leave the necessary legislation to be passed by Member States, for example, in the fields of customs duties, agriculture and transport. For this purpose complex legislation would be needed immediately on joining the Communities; and further legislation would be needed from time to time to give effect to subsequent Community instruments. Legislation of this character poses no new problem. The necessary provisions would be enacted by Parliament, or possibly by delegated legislation issued under Parliamentary authority which could cover future as well as present Community instruments.

22. Secondly, it would be necessary to pass legislation giving the force of law to those provisions of the Treaties and Community instruments which are intended to take direct internal effect within the Member States. This legislation would be needed, because, under our constitutional law, adherence to a treaty does not of itself have the effect of changing our internal law even where provisions of the treaty are intended to have direct internal effect as law within the participating States. The legislation would have to cover both provisions in force when we joined and those coming into force subsequently as a result of instruments issued by the Community institutions. No new problem would be created by the provisions which were in force at the time we became a member of the Communities. The constitutional innovation would lie in the acceptance in advance as part of the law of the United Kingdom of provisions to be made in the future by instruments issued by the Community institutions—a situation for which there is no precedent in this country. However, these instruments, like ordinary delegated legislation, would derive their force under the law of the United Kingdom from the original enactment passed by Parliament.

Impact on United Kingdom Law

23. The Community law having direct internal effect is designed to take precedence over the domestic law of the Member States. From this it follows that the legislation of the Parliament of the United Kingdom giving effect to that law would have to do so in such a way as to override existing national law so far as inconsistent with it. This result need not be left to implication, and it would be open to Parliament to enact from time to time any necessary consequential amendments or repeals. It would also follow that within the fields occupied by the Community law Parliament would have to refrain from passing fresh legislation

inconsistent with that law as for the time being in force. This would not however involve any constitutional innovation. Many of our treaty obligations already impose such restraints—for example, the Charter of the United Nations, the European Convention on Human Rights and GATT.

24. The legislative powers granted to the Community institutions are in any event limited to the purposes laid down in Articles 2 and 3 of the EEC Treaty, Articles 2 and 3 of the ECSC Treaty and Articles 1 and 2 of the EURATOM Treaty, which are mainly economic purposes. Within that general framework, the different sections of the Treaties usually contain a statement of objects, and the specific law-making powers are defined by reference to particular purposes set out in the relevant provisions of the Treaties. By the terms of the Treaties themselves neither the objects nor the particular purposes can be extended except by unanimous agreement and any revision of the Treaties to this end requires ratification by all Member States in accordance with their respective constitutional requirements: see Articles 235 and 236 of the EEC Treaty, and virtually identical provisions of the other Treaties.[10]

25. Moreover, Community law operates only in the fields covered by the Treaties, that is, broadly: customs duties; agriculture; free movement of labour, services and capital; transport; monopolies and restrictive practices; state aid for industry; and the regulation of the coal and steel and nuclear energy industries. By far the greater part of our domestic law would remain unchanged. Nothing in Community law would, for example, materially affect the general principles of our criminal law, or those of the law of contract or tort or its Scottish equivalent, nor would it affect the land law, the relations of landlord and tenant, housing and town and country planning law, matrimonial law or the law of inheritance. It is also important to bear in mind the distinction between those provisions of Community law which have direct internal effect within the Member States, and those which do not, even though it cannot yet be said precisely where the line between the two is to be drawn. That it is the former that are most significant from the point of view of national law has already been indicated. First, because Community provisions which have direct internal effect would fall to be considered by the United Kingdom courts and would present them with problems of interpretation and questions of the relationship between the Community law and our ordinary national law. Secondly, because it is in the field of Community law having direct internal effect that persons and undertakings within the United Kingdom would be subject to penalties imposed directly by the Community institutions. It is therefore useful to examine some general questions posed by the impact of the provisions having direct internal effect.

26. The principal fields in which provisions of this kind are so far to be found are restrictive practices and monopolies, movement of workers and social security of migrant workers, agriculture, transport, and the regulation of the coal and steel and nuclear energy industries. The nature of these matters dispels the idea that the continental origin of the relevant provisions would necessarily make them difficult to apply

in the United Kingdom. In the United Kingdom legislation on matters of this kind has been framed in virtually identical terms for England and Scotland and has fitted with equal aptitude into both legal systems despite the antithesis between the common law tradition of the former and the Roman law associations of the latter. For example, the Restrictive Trade Practices Act 1956 does no violence to either system in spite of differences in the law of contract in the two countries.

27. The structure of the Treaties and of the regulations and other instruments issued by the authorities of Communities differs from that of statutes and subordinate legislation in the United Kingdom; provisions are framed in more general terms and more is left to judicial interpretation. For this reason the interpretation of law emanating from the Communities would present some problems to the legal profession and, so far as it fell within their jurisdiction, to the courts of the United Kingdom. The task of construing international agreements given the force of law in the United Kingdom would not, however, be a new one. United Kingdom courts, when construing such documents, have regard to the fact that their character and drafting differs from that of United Kingdom legislation. Moreover, if the United Kingdom became a member of the Communities we would be taking part in the preparation of future Community instruments and the special needs of our legal system would be taken into account.

28. So far as they had difficulties of interpretation, United Kingdom courts should, in the course of time, derive a good deal of assistance from the body of decisions given by the European Court on references under Article 177 of the EEC Treaty and Article 150 of the EURATOM Treaty. Edited Reports of the important case law of the European Communities are already available in this country. On the United Kingdom joining the Communities, United Kingdom courts would be enabled, and in the case of final courts would be required, to refer any questions raised before them on the interpretation of the EEC or EURATOM Treaties to the European Court for a ruling. Thus provisions of Community law raising difficulties in their application to our legal system would in time become clarified by decisions of the European Court. In giving its judgments on references under Article 177 the European Court limits itself to giving abstract rulings on the meaning of the relevant provisions of the Treaties and their instruments and leaves it to the national court to apply the provisions so interpreted to the particular circumstances of the case.

29. It may be assumed that there would be an official and authoritative English version of the Treaties[11] and their instruments, both present and future. This would be the primary version for use by United Kingdom courts and, in the case of future instruments, would be published in the Official Journal of the Communities. It would probably be convenient to make provision for publication of the Treaties and regulations in this country by the Stationery Office.

30. Most of the Community law having direct internal effect, in so far as it imposes obligations, does so in relation to industrial and commercial activities and does not touch citizens in their private capacities.

This is true even of the agriculture regulations, which regulate an industry operated mainly by individual farmers. So far as the Community law directly affects individuals in their private capacities it confers rights rather than imposes obligations. The jurisprudence of the European Court indicates, for example, that private individuals may be able to rely on provisions of the Community law in contesting the imposition of customs duties alleged to be contrary to a Treaty provision. There is therefore no reason to think that the impact of Community law would weaken or destroy any of the basic rights and liberties of individuals under the law of the United Kingdom. The only regulations directly affecting individuals in their private capacities (apart from those concerned with the terms of service of employees etc., of the Community institutions) are those which facilitate the free movement of labour by entitling workers to take up available employment in other Member countries and by giving reciprocal rights under the social security systems of the different Member States to workers moving from one country to another. This would not be likely to affect the rights of persons who stay in this country under the social security legislation (including the Health Services) of the United Kingdom and even for those who sought employment abroad there would be little change from the position under the present reciprocal agreements with the individual Members of the Six. It is also noteworthy that the EEC regulations on these subjects which affect private individuals fall primarily to be administered and enforced by the domestic authorities and tribunals of the Member States.

31. In general, responsibility for the enforcement of the Community law having direct internal effect (and indeed of Community law as a whole) lies with the Commission or the High Authority. These institutions have power in some cases to decide whether there has been an infringement and, in accordance with a quasi-judicial procedure, to impose penalties[12] for the infringement: see for examples Articles 3, 16 and 19 of EEC Regulation 17 (Restrictive Practices) and Articles 36 and 64 of the ECSC Treaty. Such a decision is subject to challenge before the European Court in proceedings under Article 173 of the EEC Treaty, and the imposition of a penalty has always been made subject to a right of appeal to the court under Article 172: there are similar provisions in the other Treaties.

32. This enforcement procedure has given rise to anxieties that British subjects would be liable to criminal proceedings in which they would not enjoy the safeguards of the criminal law and procedure of this country. Such anxieties appear to be based on misconceptions. In the first place, as already stated, the powers are not applicable to persons in their private capacities, and there are no provisions, such as are often found in United Kingdom statutes, making directors and officers of a company personally liable for breaches. Secondly, the procedures which lead to the imposition of penalties under the existing Community provisions are not regarded under Community law as criminal proceedings, so that trial by the ordinary criminal processes would not be appropriate. Important safeguards are that before imposing a penalty the Commission or High Authority are required to give the party concerned an oppor-

tunity to state his case and that there is a right of appeal to the European Court. The appeal procedure ensures a fair and full hearing before an impartial tribunal of the highest judicial quality. Further, if an individual or undertaking in a Member State wishes to challenge a decision on any of the grounds[13] set out in Article 173 of the EEC Treaty, the Member State can become a party to the proceedings and thus ensure a thorough ventilation of any complaint of an abuse of power by the institution concerned.

33. In some cases the Treaty or regulation requires the Member State to provide penalties under its own domestic legislation for breaches of Community law. The fact that the sanctions imposed by Community provisions are of a civil character suggests that the penalties provided by the national law should be of the same character. It would therefore be appropriate to provide monetary penalties recoverable by a civil rather than a criminal process (similar to the fines and penalties under the Income Tax Acts, which by virtue of section 56(3) of the Finance Act 1960 are recoverable by civil proceedings in the High Court, or in Scotland, the Court of Session). The only exception would be for cases in which the breach consisted in the furnishing of false information. It may have to be recognised, however, that to avoid undue disparities between penalties provided by the various Member States some harmonisation will be necessary in this field.

34. The Commission or the High Authority, as the case may be, are in certain instances, empowered by the three Treaties to authorise their own inspectors to enter premises, inspect books, premises and vehicles and interrogate persons, and the Member State on whose territory the powers are exercised is in each case enabled to insist on its own officials co-operating with the Commission's or High Authority's officials in the exercise of the powers. In the event of compulsion being necessary, the Member State is required to lend its assistance. Except in the case of inspections for purposes of security control in the nuclear energy field, where Article 81 of the EURATOM Treaty provides for the issue of a warrant by the President of the European court, it should be open to the United Kingdom to provide that compulsory powers should not be exercised except in pursuance of an order made by the United Kingdom court. In any event, except for the purposes of security control in the nuclear energy field, the Community institutions rely mainly on information obtained for them by the authorities of the Member States or on voluntary co-operation of the industries or undertakings concerned.

HARMONISATION AND APPROXIMATION OF LAWS

35. Some mention must be made of the Articles of the EEC Treaty dealing with harmonisation and approximation of laws. Article 99 empowers the Council acting on proposals by the Commission to take action for harmonising the legislation of Member States concerning turnover taxes, excise duties and other forms of indirect taxation. Article 100 covers such legislative and administrative provisions of Member States as affect directly the establishment or functioning of the

Common Market. Under both Articles the scope for the creation of Community law is therefore confined to the economic and financial field. National interests are safeguarded because a decision under Article 99 and a directive under Article 100 can only be made on a unanimous vote of the Council, and under Article 100 the Assembly and the Economic and Social Committee must be consulted in the case of directives involving any amendment of national legislation. Article 101, which enables directives to be issued by the Council on a qualified majority vote, is limited to the rectification of a discrepancy in the legislative or administrative provisions of Member States which is found to be interfering with competition within the Common Market and consequently producing distortion which needs to be eliminated. Under Article 100 a number of directives of a technical character relating to such matters as public health and pharmaceutical classifications have been issued; use has been made of Article 99 in the field of transport taxation and turnover taxes; the power conferred by Article 101 has never yet been used.

36. Article 220 requires Member States to enter into negotiations with each other to regulate, in the interests of their nationals, a number of matters touching on the establishment of the Common Market. These include the abolition of double taxation, mutual recognition of the status of firms and companies and of their ability to transfer their seat from one country to another or to enter into mergers, and the enforcement of civil judgments. Negotiations presently proceeding in these and allied subjects include some matters which although of Community interest fall outside the scope of the EEC Treaty. Conventions resulting from any of these negotiations will not, strictly, derive their legal force from the EEC Treaty, but any new member joining the Common Market would no doubt be expected to accede to them. Work is in progress on the creation of a European type of company, the creation of a European patent, the creation of a European trade-mark, a convention on bankruptcy and an agreement on jurisdictional competence and the enforcement of civil judgments. Only the last mentioned project is nearing completion. Work on the rest is still in a preliminary stage. Considerable amendment of our national law might eventually be involved; but these are subjects in which, whether we join the European Community or not, we would expect a movement towards greater international assimilation of laws.

37. The draft European Convention on jurisdictional competence and enforcement of judgements[14] expressly provides that any new member of the Community will be required to accept the Convention as a basis for the negotiations which are obligatory to implement the relevant part of Article 220 of the Treaty. The Convention goes considerably further than the bilateral conventions on enforcement of judgments which we have hitherto concluded: it covers the power of a court to entertain actions against foreign-domiciled defendants as well as the recognition of any judgment emanating from the court. Accession to this convention would oblige us to abandon some jurisdiction hitherto exercised by our courts and to give effect to certain classes of foreign

judgments, particularly those concerning maintenance and affiliation obligations, which are not at present enforceable in this country.

TREATY RELATIONS OUTSIDE THE COMMUNITIES

38. The preceding paragraphs of this paper have been concerned with the legal impact of the European Treaties on United Kingdom national law. Joining the Communities would, however, have important consequences for our international legal position.

39. By becoming a party to the Treaties we should be restricted in future international dealings by the need not to violate any of the obligations imposed upon us by those Treaties. In addition membership of the EEC would in certain respects affect our treaty-making powers and freedom of negotiation in more direct ways, and would also have consequences for our existing treaty commitments.

40. As regards commercial policy, Articles 110 to 116 of the EEC Treaty, read with Article 228, contain provisions that limit considerably the freedom of Members to negotiate agreements. They envisage that during the transitional period (the terminal date of which cannot under Article 8 of the EEC Treaty be later than the end of 1972) the Commission will conduct all tariff negotiations on behalf of the Member States with third countries about the common customs tariff, subject to supervision by the Council acting during the first two stages of the transitional period by unanimity and subsequently by qualified majority vote. After expiry of the transitional period, the Commission will *inter alia* negotiate tariff or trade agreements with third countries subject to supervision by the Council acting by qualified majority vote. Any such agreements are to be concluded by the Council on behalf of Member States of the Community acting eventually by qualified majority vote.

41. Furthermore, within the framework of any international organisation of an economic character (e.g. OECD, World Bank, IMF) Member States, as from the end of the transitional period, may only proceed, in matters of particular interest to the Common Market, by way of common action, the scope and implementation of which are to be determined by the Council acting by means of a qualified majority. During the transitional period the obligation is only to consult together with a view to concerting action and adopting as far as possible a uniform attitude (Article 116).

42. Entry into the Common Market would also affect the exercise of our rights and obligations under existing Treaties. Article 234 of the EEC Treaty provides that the provisions of that Treaty shall not affect rights and obligations arising from prior agreements between a Member State and a non-Member State, but if such prior agreement is incompatible with the Treaty the Member State is obliged to take all appropriate steps to eliminate any proven incompatibilities. Furthermore Article 224 states that Member States shall consult one another with a view to taking in common the necessary steps to avoid the operation of the Common Market being affected by measures which a Member State may be called upon to take in case of serious internal disturbances

affecting public policy or the maintenance of law and order (*ordre public*), in case of war or serious international tension constituting a threat of war, or in order to carry out undertakings into which it has entered for the purpose of maintaining peace and international security.

NORTHERN IRELAND

43. This Paper relates to the United Kingdom generally, but a special problem arises in relation to Northern Ireland, by reason of the limitations on the powers of the Northern Ireland Parliament. Section 4 of the Government of Ireland Act 1920 prevents that Parliament from legislating in respect of Treaties, even though the subject is one on which it is empowered to legislate for domestic purposes. There would be a number of matters of this kind requiring legislation which would more appropriately be dealt with by the Northern Ireland Parliament than by the United Kingdom Parliament, e.g. in the field of social security; to make this possible new enabling provisions would have to be enacted to overcome the restrictions on the powers of the Northern Ireland Parliament.

NOTES

[* This material was first published in 1967 as Command Paper Cmnd. 3301 and is reproduced with the permission of the Controller of H.M. Stationery Office.]

[1] References in this paper to 'the Council' are intended, if the context is a general one, to cover each of the three Councils of Ministers, and similarly references to 'the Commission' are intended to cover the EEC Commission and the EURATOM Commission.

[2] The Treaty of Fusion repeals and amends certain provisions of the Treaties setting up the European Communities (see Articles 7, 8, 19, 21, 23, 24 and 26–28). These amendments are consequential upon the amalgamation of the institutions but otherwise do not alter materially the provisions of the Treaties. Since the Treaty is not yet in force these amendments have been ignored for the purposes of this paper. When the Treaty has been ratified an English translation will be published by the Stationery Office.

[3] The exception is under Article 95 of the ECSC Treaty, which provides for limited amendment of the powers of the High Authority on a joint proposal of that body and the Council. The ultimate power of approving such amendments lies with the European Parliament: see fourth paragraph of Article 95.

[4] There is an exception in the case of Article 54 (which deals with investment programmes for coal and steel). An opinion issued under the fourth paragraph by the High Authority is given the force of a decision by the fifth paragraph, in the circumstances there specified.

[5] See Article 148 of the EEC Treaty, which gives 4 votes each to France,

Germany and Italy, 2 votes each to Belgium and the Netherlands, and 1 vote to Luxembourg.

[6] The Council does have some power of taking decisions; e.g. under Articles 59 and 72.

[7] Paragraph 2 of Article 8 of the Treaty of Fusion amends in certain respects the voting procedures set out in Article 28.

[8] For examples of cases in which decisions of Community institutions have been annulled see *Ferriere e Acciaierie Napoletane* v. *High Authority,* 1966 Common Market Law Reports p. 211, *Toepfer K. G. etc.* v. *E.E.C. Commission,* 1966 Common Market Law Reports p. 111.

[9] Under the ECSC Treaty reference is obligatory for all courts.

[10] The only exception to this is that under the ECSC Treaty there is a limited power to amend the powers of the High Authority, exercisable jointly by the High Authority and the Council subject to an opinion of the European Court and to the subsequent approval of the European Parliament: see Article 95 of the Treaty.

[11] Except perhaps in the case of the ECSC Treaty, where the French text is the only official version and where it might therefore only be possible to have an unofficial English version. Unofficial translations have already been published by the Stationery Office...

[12] These penalties, except in the case of the EURATOM Treaty, are always monetary.

[13] The grounds are 'lack of jurisdiction, infringements of important procedural rules of this Treaty or of any rule of law relating to its implementation, or misuse of powers'. See also Article 146 of the EURATOM Treaty and Article 33 of the ECSC Treaty.

[[14] Convention on Jurisdiction and the Enforcement of Civil and Commercial Judgments, signed 27 September 1968. Text in Campbell, *op. cit.,* Supp. 1970, p. 157.]

Appendix 2

THE EUROPEAN ECONOMIC COMMUNITY

FIRST DIRECTIVE OF THE COUNCIL[1]

of 9 March 1968

with a view to co-ordinating, in order to render of equal value the safeguards which Member States require of companies and firms within the meaning of the second paragraph of Article 58 of the Treaty, so as to protect the interests of both members and outsiders

(68/151/EEC)

THE COUNCIL OF THE EUROPEAN COMMUNITIES,

HAVING REGARD to the Treaty setting up the European Economic Community and in particular Article 54(3)(g) thereof:

HAVING REGARD to the general programme for the abolition of restrictions on the right of establishment[2] and in particular Part VI thereof;

HAVING REGARD to the Proposal of the Commission;

HAVING REGARD to the Opinion of the Assembly;[3]

HAVING REGARD to the Opinion of the Economic and Social Committee;[4]

WHEREAS the co-ordination provided for in Article 54(3)(g) and in the general programme for the abolition of restrictions on the right of establishment is urgent, especially in regard to Sociétés par actions (companies limited by shares) and Sociétés à responsabilité limitée (private companies), since the operations of such companies often extend beyond their national frontiers;

WHEREAS the co-ordination of national provisions concerning publication, the validity or invalidity of undertakings entered into by such companies, takes on a special importance, particularly from the point of view of ensuring the protection of the interests of third parties;

WHEREAS in such fields Community provisions must be adopted simultaneously for such companies, since the only safeguards they offer to third parties are their assets;

WHEREAS publicity must be provided to afford to third parties knowledge of the fundamental documents of constitution of the company and certain information about them, in particular the identity of the persons authorised to act on their behalf;

WHEREAS the protection of third parties must be ensured by provisions limiting, as far as possible, the causes of avoidance of liabilities undertaken in the name of the company;

WHEREAS it is necessary, with a view to ensuring legal security in relations between a company or firm and third parties as well as between members, to limit the number of grounds on which a company or firm may be declared illegal and on the retrospective effect of the declaration of illegality and to fix a short period of time for any third party objection which may be taken thereto;

HAS ADOPTED THIS DIRECTIVE:

Article 1

The measures of co-ordination laid down in this Directive shall apply to the legal, statutory and administrative provisions of the Member States relating to the forms of the following companies or firms (hereinafter referred to as 'companies'):

For Germany:

die Aktiengesellschaft, die Kommanditgesellschaft auf Aktien, die Gesellschaft mit beschränkter Haftung;

For Belgium:

de naamloze vennootschap, de commanditaire vennootschap op aandelen, de personenvennootschap met beperkte aansprakelijkheid;

la société anonyme, la société en commandite par actions, la société de personnes à responsabilité limitée;

For France:

la société anonyme, la société en commandite par actions, la société à responsabilité limitée;

For Italy:

società per azioni, società in accomandita per azioni, società a responsabilità limitata;

For Luxembourg:

la société anonyme, la société en commandite par actions, la société à responsabilité limitée;

For the Netherlands:

de naamloze vennootschap, de commanditaire vennootschap op aandelen.

SECTION I. PUBLICATION TO BE EFFECTED

Article 2

(1) Member States shall take the necessary measures to ensure the compulsory publication by companies of the following documents and particulars at least:

(*a*) the document constituting the company and its statutes if they are contained in a separate instrument;

(*b*) any amendments to the documents mentioned in (*a*), including any provision for continuation of existence;
(*c*) after each amendment of the document of constitution or the statutes, the complete text of the instrument as amended up to date;
(*d*) the appointment, relinquishment of office and identity of the persons who, either as a body legally constituted, or as members of such a body:

(i) are authorised to act for and on behalf of the company towards third parties and to represent it in legal proceedings,
(ii) take part in the administration, supervision or control of the company.

Such publication must clearly state whether the persons authorised to act for and on behalf of the company may do so alone or must act jointly.

(*e*) at intervals of no more than one year the amount of the capital subscribed, when the document of constitution or the statutes mention an authorised capital, unless every increase in the capital subscribed gives rise to an amendment of the statutes;
(*f*) the balance sheet and the profit and loss account for each financial period. The document containing the balance sheet must show the identity of the persons who, in accordance with law, are authorised to certify it. However, in respect of *sociétés à responsabilité limitée* (private limited liability companies) under German, Belgian, French, Italian or Luxembourg law, mentioned in Article 1, and the *sociétés anonymes fermées* (closed companies limited by shares) under Netherlands law, the compulsory application of this provision shall be postponed until the date on which a Directive is put into effect on the co-ordination of the contents of balance sheets and profit and loss accounts and dispensing with the necessity to publish all or part of the said documents of such companies whose balance is below a figure which it will fix in a directive. The Council shall adopt such a Directive within two years following the adoption of the present Directive;
(*g*) change of address of the registered office;
(*h*) the dissolution of the company;
(*i*) any decision of a court pronouncing the invalidation of the company;
(*j*) the appointment and the identity of any liquidators and their respective powers, unless such powers are expressly and exclusively derived from the law or from the statutes;
(*k*) the termination of the liquidation and the deletion from the register in Member States where such liquidation may give rise to legal consequences.

(2) For the purposes of paragraph 1 (*f*) companies which fulfil the following conditions shall be considered as closed companies limited by shares (*sociétés anonymes fermées*):

(*a*) they must not issue bearer shares;

(*b*) no 'certificate to the holder of registered shares' (*certificat au porteur d'actions nominatives*) within the meaning of Article 42(*c*) of the Netherlands commercial code may be transferred by any person whatsoever;
(*c*) the shares may not be quoted on the stock exchange;
(*d*) the statutes shall contain a clause requiring the approval of the company for the transfer of shares to third parties, excepting in the case of transfers arising from death and, if the statutes so provide, in the case of transfers to a spouse, forebears and issue; to the exclusion of any transfers in blank, each transfer must be made in writing under hand, signed by the transferor or transferee or by means of an official record;
(*e*) the statutes shall show the nature of the closed company limited by shares (*société anonyme fermée*); the name of the company shall include the words 'Besloten Naamloze Vennootschap' or the initials 'B.N.V.'

Article 3

(1) In each Member State a file shall be opened at either a central register or a trade register or register of companies and firms, for each of the companies inscribed therein.
(2) Every document and all the particulars which must be published by virtue of Article 2 shall be entered in the file or transcribed in the register; the purpose of the entries in the register must in any case appear in the file.
(3) A complete or abridged copy of any document or particular referred to in Article 2 must be obtainable by application in writing at a price not exceeding its administrative cost.

Copies sent out shall be certified as 'true copies', unless the applicant dispenses with such certification.
(4) The documents and particulars referred to in paragraph 2 shall be published in the national publication specially appointed for the purpose by the Member State, either in full or abridged, or in the form of a reference to the document having been placed in the file or entered in the register.
(5) The documents and particulars may be relied on by the company as against third parties only after their publication in accordance with paragraph 4, unless the company proves that any such third party had knowledge thereof. However, with regard to transactions taking place before the sixteenth day following such publication, the documents and particulars shall not be relied upon as against third parties who prove that it was impossible for them to have had knowledge of their existence.
(6) Member States shall take the necessary measures to avoid any divergence between what is published in the press and in the register or file.

However, in cases of divergence, the text published in the press may not be relied on as against third parties; the latter may nevertheless take advantage thereof, unless the company proves that they had knowledge of the entries in the file or the register.

(7) Third parties may, moreover, always take advantage of any documents and particulars which have not yet been published, unless in the absence of publication they are not to have effect.

Article 4

Member States shall prescribe that orders given by letter or otherwise in writing shall contain a reference to the following matters:

—the register with which the file mentioned in Article 3 is kept together with the registration number of the company in that register;
—the nature of the company, the situation of its registered office and, where appropriate, the fact that it is in liquidation.

If mention is made in the documents of the capital of the company, reference must be made to the capital subscribed and paid up.

Article 5

Each Member State shall determine the persons required to effect publication.

Article 6

Member States shall provide for appropriate penalties in case of:

—failure to publish the balance sheet and profit and loss account as laid down in Article 2(1)(*f*);
—omission of the compulsory particulars from commercial documents as provided for in Article 4.

SECTION II. VALIDITY OF COMMITMENTS ENTERED INTO BY A COMPANY

Article 7

If transactions have been carried out in the name of a company in formation before it has become a legal entity and if the company does not take over the liabilities arising from such transactions, the persons who carried them out shall be jointly and severally responsible therefor, unless otherwise agreed.

Article 8

The publication of the names of persons authorised to act for and on behalf of the company shall constitute a bar to any irregularity in their appointment being relied upon as against third parties unless the company proves that such third parties had knowledge thereof.

Article 9

(1) The company shall be liable to third parties in respect of transactions carried out by its authorised officers, even if such transactions are unconnected with the objects of the company, unless the said transactions exceed the powers that the law confers or allows to be conferred on such authorised officers.

However, Member States may provide that the company shall not be liable when such transactions are outside the objects of the company, if it proves that the third party knew that the transaction went beyond those objects or could not be unaware of it, in view of the circumstances, except that for this purpose publication of the statutes shall not by itself be sufficient to constitute such proof.
(2) The limits on the powers of the authorised officers of the company, arising under the statutes or from a decision by the competent authorities may not be relied upon as against third parties, even if they have been published.
(3) If the national law provides that the authority to represent a company may, by derogation from the rule of law on the subject, be conferred by the statutes on a single person or on several persons acting jointly, that law may provide that such a provision in the statutes may be relied on as against third parties provided that it relates to the general power of representation; reliance on such a provision in the statutes as against third parties shall be governed by the provisions of Article 3.

SECTION III. INVALIDATION OF THE COMPANY

Article 10

In all the Member States whose laws do not provide for a preventive administrative or legal control at the time of the constitution, the document of constitution and the statutes of the company as well as the amendments to such documents must be made in the form of an official record.

Article 11

The laws of the Member States may not provide for the invalidation of companies otherwise than in accordance with the following conditions:

(1) The invalidation must be ordered by the decision of a court of law;
(2) The only grounds on which invalidation may be pronounced shall be:

(*a*) non-existence of a document of constitution or failure to comply either with the rules of preventive control or with the legal requirements as to form;
(*b*) that the objects of the company are unlawful or contrary to public policy (ordre public);
(*c*) that the document of constitution or the statutes, contain no reference to the name of the company, the contributions made, the amount of the subscribed capital or the objects of the company;
(*d*) the non-observance of the provisions of the national law concerning the minimum amount of the capital, which is to be paid up;
(*e*) the incapacity of all the founder members;
(*f*) that, contrary to national law governing companies, the number of founder members is less than two.

Apart from the above cases of invalidation the existence of a company shall not be declared null and void absolutely or partially or declared voidable on any grounds whatever.

Article 12

(1) The reliance on a decision of a court of law pronouncing invalidation as against third parties shall be governed by the provisions of Article 3. Objection by a third party, when provided for under the national law, shall only be admissible within a period of six months from the publication of the decision of the court.
(2) Invalidation shall bring about the liquidation of the company, in the same way as dissolution.
(3) Invalidation shall not of itself affect the validity of any commitments entered into by the company nor of those made with it, subject to the effects of liquidation.
(4) The laws of each Member State may govern the effects of invalidation between members of a company.
(5) Holders of shares shall remain bound to pay subscribed capital not paid up, in so far as arrangements made with creditors so require.

SECTION IV. GENERAL

Article 13

Member States shall bring into force, within a period of eighteen months from the notification of this Directive, all amendments to their legislative or administrative provisions necessary to conform with its provisions and inform the Commission thereof immediately.

The obligation to effect publication provided for in Article 2(1)(*f*) shall only come into force thirty months after notification of this Directive, in respect of *sociétés anonymes* (companies limited by shares) coming under Netherlands law other than those referred to in the present Article 42(*c*) of the Netherlands commercial code.

Member States may provide that the publication of the full text of the statutes, in wording resulting from the amendments made since the constitution of the company, shall not be required before the occasion of the next amendment to the statutes or, failing that, not later than 31 December 1970.

Member States shall make certain to notify the Commission of the text of the main provisions of domestic law they adopt on the subject matter of this Directive.

Article 14

This Directive is addressed to all Member States.

Done at Brussels, 9 March 1968
By the Council
The President
M. COUVE DE MURVILLE

APPENDIX 2

NOTES

[1] Foreign and Commonwealth Office translation. (French original in *Official Journal* No. L 65, 14 March 1968, p. 65/8.)
[2] O.J. No. 2 of 15 January 1962, p. 36/62.
[3] O.J. No. 96 of 28 May 1966, p. 1519/66.
[4] O.J. No. 194 of 27 November 1964, p. 3248/64.

Appendix 3

COUNCIL REGULATION No. 17

First implementing regulation pursuant to Articles 85 and 86 of the Treaty as amended by Council Regulation N° 59 of 3 July 1962.[1]

Article 1

Basic provision

The agreements, decisions and concerted practices referred to in Article 85, paragraph 1, of the Treaty and any abuse of a dominant position on the market within the meaning of Article 86 of the Treaty shall be prohibited, no prior decision to this effect being required; Articles 6, 7 and 23 of the present Regulation shall not be affected by this provision.

Article 2

Negative clearance

At the request of the enterprises or associations of enterprises concerned, the Commission may find that, according to the information it has obtained, there are, under Article 85, paragraph 1, or Article 86 of the Treaty, no grounds for it to intervene with respect to an agreement, decision or practice.

Article 3

Ending of infringements

1. If, acting on request or ex officio, the Commission finds that an enterprise or association of enterprises is infringing Article 85 or Article 86 of the Treaty, it can by means of a decision oblige the enterprises or associations of enterprises concerned to put an end to such infringement.
2. A request to this effect may be submitted by:

(*a*) Member States;
(*b*) Natural and legal persons and associations of persons, who show a justified interest.

3. Without prejudice to the other provisions of the present Regulation, the Commission, before taking the decision mentioned in paragraph 1,

---

[1] The amendments introduced by Regulation N° 59 are underlined.

N.B. Forms to be used under these Regulations may be obtained from the Association of British Chambers of Commerce 68 Queen Street London E.C.4. The explanatory manual for firms may be obtained from The Information Service of the European Communities 23 Chesham St. London S.W.1.

may address to the enterprises or associations of enterprises concerned recommendations designed to put an end to the infringement.

Article 4

Notification of new agreements, decisions and practices

1. The Commission shall be notified of any agreement, decisions or concerted practices referred to in Article 85, paragraph 1, of the Treaty which have come into being after the entry into force of the present Regulation and for which those concerned wish to invoke Article 85, paragraph 3. As long as such notification has not taken place, no decision to issue a declaration under Article 85, paragraph 1, may be rendered.
2. Paragraph 1 shall not be applicable to agreements, decisions and concerted practices where:

(1) enterprises of only one Member State take part and where such agreements, decisions and practices involve neither imports nor exports between Member States;
(2) only two enterprises take part and the sole effect of these agreements is:

(*a*) to restrict the freedom of one party to the contract to fix prices or conditions of trading in the resale of goods which have been acquired from the other party to the contract, or
(*b*) to impose restraint on the exercise of the rights of any person acquiring or using industrial property rights—particularly patents, utility models, registered designs or trade marks—or on the exercise of the rights of any person entitled, under a contract, to acquire or use manufacturing processes or knowledge relating to the utilisation or application of industrial techniques;

(3) their sole object is:

(*a*) the development or the uniform application of standards and types,
(*b*) joint research to improve techniques, provided that the result is accessible to all parties and that each of them can exploit it.

The Commission may be notified of such agreements, decisions and practices.

Article 5

Notification of existing agreements, decisions and practices

1. The Commission must be notified *before 1 November 1962*, of any agreements, decisions and concerted practices referred to in Article 85, paragraph 1, of the Treaty which are already in existence at the date of entry into force of the present Regulation and in respect of which those concerned wish to invoke Article 85, paragraph 3, of the Treaty. *Provided always that not withstanding the foregoing provision, any*

agreements, decisions and concerted practices to which not more than two enterprises are parties must be notified before 1 February 1963.
2. Paragraph 1 is not applicable where the said agreements, decisions and concerted practices fall within the categories referred to in paragraph 2 of Article 4; the Commission may be notified of these.

Article 6

Decisions to issue a declaration under Article 85, paragraph 3

1. When the Commission decides to issue a declaration under Article 85, paragraph 3, it shall indicate the date from which the decision shall take effect. This date shall not be prior to the date of notification.
2. The second sentence of paragraph 1 shall not be applicable to the agreements, decisions and concerted practices referred to in Article 4, paragraph 2, and Article 5, paragraph 2, nor to those which are referred to in Article 5, paragraph 1, and of which the Commission has been notified within the time-limit fixed therein.

Article 7

Special provisions for existing agreements, decisions and practices

1. Where agreements, decisions and concerted practices already in existence at the date of the entry into force of the present Regulation and of which the Commission has been notified *within the time-limits set out in Article 5, paragraph 1,* do not meet the requirements of Article 85, paragraph 3, of the Treaty, and where the enterprises and associations of enterprises concerned put an end to them or modify them so that they no longer fall under the prohibition laid down in Article 85, paragraph 1, or so that they then meet the requirements of Article 85, paragraph 3, the prohibition laid down in Article 85, paragraph 1, shall be applicable only for a period fixed by the Commission. A decision by the Commission pursuant to the foregoing sentence cannot be invoked against enterprises or associations of enterprises which have not given their express assent to the notification.
2. Paragraph 1 shall be applicable to agreements, decisions and concerted practices which are already in existence at the date of the entry into force of the present Regulation and which fall within the categories referred to in Article 4, paragraph 2, provided that notification shall have taken place before 1 January 1964.

Article 8

Period of validity and revoking of decisions to issue a declaration under Article 85, paragraph 3

1. A decision to issue a declaration under Article 85, paragraph 3, of the Treaty shall be valid for a specified period and may have certain conditions and stipulations attached.
2. The decision may be renewed on request provided that the conditions laid down in Article 85, paragraph 3, of the Treaty continue to be fulfilled.
3. The Commission may revoke or alter its decision or prohibit those concerned from taking certain courses of action:

(*a*) where the de facto situation has changed with respect to a factor essential in the granting of the decision,
(*b*) where those concerned infringe a stipulation attached to the decision,
(*c*) where the decision is based on false information or has been obtained fraudulently, or
(*d*) where those concerned abuse the exemption from the provisions of Article 85, paragraph 1, of the Treaty granted to them by the decision.

In the cases covered by sub-paragraphs (*b*), (*c*) and (*d*), the decision can also be revoked with retroactive effect.

Article 9

Competence

1. Subject to review of its decision by the Court of Justice, the Commission shall have sole competence to declare Article 85, paragraph 1, inapplicable pursuant to Article 85, paragraph 3, of the Treaty.
2. The Commission shall have competence to apply Article 85, paragraph 1, and Article 86 of the Treaty, even if the time-limits for notification laid down in Article 5, paragraph 1, and Article 7, paragraph 2, have not expired.
3. As long as the Commission has not initiated any procedure pursuant to Articles 2, 3 or 6, the authorities of the Member States shall remain competent to apply Article 85, paragraph 1, and Article 86 in accordance with Article 88 of the Treaty, even if the time-limits for notification laid down in Article 5, paragraph 1, and Article 7 have not expired.

Article 10

Liaison with the authorities of the Member States

1. The Commission shall transmit without delay to the competent authorities of the Member States copies of the requests, applications and notifications together with copies of the most important documents

which have been sent to it with the purpose of establishing the existence of infringements of Article 85 or Article 86 of the Treaty, or with the purpose of obtaining negative clearance or a decision to issue a declaration under Article 85, paragraph 3.

2. It shall carry out the procedures mentioned in paragraph 1 in close and constant liaison with the competent authorities of the Member States; and these authorities may submit their views on the said procedures.

3. A Consultative Committee on Cartels and Monopolies shall be consulted prior to any decision consequent upon a course of procedure referred to in paragraph 1 and prior to any decision concerning the renewal, the alteration or the revocation of a decision to issue a declaration under Article 85, paragraph 3, of the Treaty.

4. The Consultative Committee shall be composed of officials competent in the field of cartels and monopolies. Each Member State shall appoint one official to represent it, who, if he is prevented from attending, may be replaced by another official.

5. The consultation shall take place at a joint meeting called by the Commission; the session shall take place fourteen days at the earliest after dispatch of the convocation letter. This letter shall be accompanied by an exposition of the case to be considered, indicating the most important documents, and a preliminary draft of the decision shall be enclosed.

6. The Consultative Committee may tender an opinion even if some members are absent and have not been replaced by another official. The result of the consultation shall be set out in a written statement which shall be attached to the draft of the decision. It shall not be made public.

Article 11

Requests for information

1. In the execution of the duties assigned to it by Article 89 and by provisions pursuant to Article 87 of the Treaty, the Commission shall have power to seek all necessary information from the Governments and competent authorities of the Member States as well as from enterprises and associations of enterprises.

2. When sending a request for information to an enterprise or association of enterprises, the Commission shall at the same time address a copy of this request to the competent authority in the Member State in the territory of which the principal place of business of the enterprise or the association of enterprises is situated.

3. In its request the Commission shall indicate the legal basis and the purpose of the same, and the penalties for supplying false information laid down in Article 15, paragraph 1, sub-paragraph b.

4. Information must be supplied on request by the owners of the enterprises or by their representatives and in the case of legal persons, of companies or of associations without legal personality, by the persons responsible for representing them according to the law or the memorandum or articles of association.

5. Where the enterprise or association of enterprises does not supply the information required within the time-limit set by the Commission, or supplies incomplete information, the Commission's request for information shall be made by means of a decision. This decision shall specify the information requested, fix an appropriate time-limit within which it is to be supplied and specify the sanctions applicable under Article 15, paragraph 1, sub-paragraph b, and under Article 16, paragraph 1, sub-paragraph c, and shall indicate that there is a right to institute proceedings against the decision before the Court of Justice.
6. The Commission shall at the same time send a copy of its decision to the competent authority of the Member State in the territory of which the principal place of business of the enterprise or association of enterprises is situated.

Article 12

Enquiries by economic sectors

1. If in any sector of the economy the trend of trade between Member States, price movements, inflexibility of prices or other circumstances suggest that in the economic sector concerned competition is being restricted or distorted within the Common Market, the Commission may decide to conduct a general enquiry in the course of which it may request enterprises in the sector concerned to supply the information necessary for giving effect to the principles laid down in Articles 85 and 86 of the Treaty and for carrying out the tasks entrusted to the Commission.
2. The Commission may in particular request any enterprise or group of enterprises in the sector concerned to communicate to it all agreements, decisions and concerted practices which are exempted from notification by virtue of Article 4, paragraph 2, and Article 5, paragraph 2.
3. When making enquiries as provided for in paragraph 2, the Commission shall also request enterprises or groups of enterprises whose size suggest that they occupy a dominant position within the Common Market or within a substantial part thereof to supply any particulars relating to the structure of the enterprises and to the conduct of their affairs necessary to appraise their situation in the light of Article 86 of the Treaty.
4. Article 10, paragraphs 3 to 6, and Articles 11, 13 and 14 shall be applied *mutatis mutandis.*

Article 13

Investigations by authorities of the Member States

1. At the request of the Commission, the competent authorities of the Member States shall carry out the investigations which the Commission considers necessary under Article 14, paragraph 1, or which it has ordered by a decision taken pursuant to Article 14, paragraph 3. The

servants of the competent authorities of the Member States carrying out this investigation shall exercise their powers on production of a written warrant issued by the competent authority of the Member State in the territory of which the investigation is to be carried out. This warrant shall indicate the subject and the purpose of the enquiry.
2. The servants of the Commission may, at its request or at that of the competent authority of the Member State in the territory of which the investigation is to be made, assist the servants of this authority in the execution of their duties.

Article 14

Investigating powers of the Commission

1. In execution of the duties assigned to it by Article 89 and by provisions laid down pursuant to Article 87 of the Treaty, the Commission may conduct all necessary investigations into the affairs of enterprises and associations of enterprises.

To this end the servants authorized by the Commission shall be vested with the following powers:

(*a*) to examine the books and other business documents,
(*b*) to make copies of, or extracts from the same,
(*c*) to ask for verbal explanations on the spot,
(*d*) to have access to all premises, land and vehicles of enterprises.

2. The servants authorized by the Commission for these investigations shall exercise their powers on production of a written warrant stating the nature and purpose of the enquiry and the fines provided for in Article 15, paragraph 1, sub-paragraph (*c*), in the event of incomplete submission of the books or other business documents required. The Commission shall in good time advise the competent authority of the Member State in the territory of which the investigation is to take place, of this investigation, stating the name and office of the authorised servant.
3. The enterprises and associations of enterprises must submit to the investigations ordered by a decision of the Commission. The decision shall state the subject and purpose of the enquiry, fix the date when it is to begin and call attention to the sanctions provided for under Article 15, paragraph 1, sub-paragraph (*c*), and Article 16, paragraph 1, sub-paragraph (*d*), and shall indicate that there is a right to institute proceedings against the decision before the Court of Justice.
4. Before taking the decisions referred to in paragraph 3, the Commission shall consult the competent authority of the Member State in the territory of which the investigation is to be carried out.
5. The servants of the competent authority of the Member State in the territory of which the investigation is to be carried out may, at the request of this authority or of the Commission, lend assistance to the Commission's servants in the execution of their duties.
6. Where an enterprise resists an investigation ordered pursuant to the present Article, the Member State concerned shall lend the servants authorized by the Commission the assistance necessary to enable them

to carry out their investigation. The Member State shall, after consulting the Commission, take the necessary measures for this purpose before October 1 1962.

Article 15
Fines

1. The Commission may by means of a decision impose on enterprises and associations of enterprises fines of from one hundred to five thousand units of account where, wilfully or through negligence:

(*a*) they supply false or misleading information in an application submitted pursuant to Article 2 or in a notification made pursuant to Articles 4 and 5,
(*b*) they supply false information in reply to a request made pursuant to Article 11, paragraph 3 or 5, or to Article 12, or do not supply information within a time-limit fixed by a decision taken under Article 11, paragraph 5, or
(*c*) they submit in incomplete form, on the occasion of investigations carried out under Article 13 or Article 14, the books or other business documents required, or decline to submit to an investigation ordered by means of a decision taken pursuant to Article 14, paragraph 3.

2. The Commission may by means of a decision impose on enterprises and associatons of enterprises fines of from one thousand to one million units of account; this last figure may be increased to 10 per cent of the turnover of the preceding business year of each of the enterprises having taken part in the infringement, where these enterprises, wilfully or through negligence:

(*a*) have infringed the provisions of Article 85, paragraph 1, or of Article 86 of the Treaty, or
(*b*) have infringed a stipulation made under Article 8, paragraph 1.

In determining the amount of the fine the duration of the infringement shall be considered in addition to its gravity.
3. Article 10, paragraphs 3 to 6, shall apply.
4. The decisions taken under paragraphs 1 and 2 shall have no penal character.
5. The fines provided for in paragraph 2, sub-paragraph (*a*), may not be imposed for actions taking place:

(*a*) after the notification to the Commission and prior to its decision regarding the application of Article 85, paragraph 3, of the Treaty, in so far as these actions do not go beyond the limits of the activity described in the notification,
(*b*) prior to the notification of and within the framework of the agreements, decisions and concerted practices existing at the date of entry into force of the present Regulation, provided that this notification has been made within the time-limits laid down in Article 5, paragraph 1, and Article 7, paragraph 2.

6. Paragraph 5 shall not apply once the Commission has informed the enterprises concerned that after a preliminary examination it considers that the conditions of Article 85, paragraph 1, of the Treaty have been fulfilled and that application of Article 85, paragraph 3, is not warranted.

Article 16

Penalties

1. The Commission may by means of a decision impose on enterprises or associations of enterprises penalties of from fifty to one thousand units of account per day of delay, reckoned from the date fixed in its decision, in order to oblige them:

(*a*) to put an end to an infringement of Article 85 or Article 86 of the Treaty in conformity with a decision taken pursuant to Article 3,
(*b*) to discontinue any action prohibited under Article 8, paragraph 3,
(*c*) to supply completely and truthfully any information which it has requested by a decision taken under Article 11, paragraph 5,
(*d*) to submit to any investigation it has ordered by a decision taken pursuant to Article 14, paragraph 3.

2. When the enterprises or associations of enterprises have fulfilled the obligation which it was the object of the penalty to enforce, the Commission may fix the final amount of the penalty at a figure lower than that which would result from the initial decision.
3. Article 10, paragraphs 3 to 6, shall apply.

Article 17

Review by the Court of Justice

The Court of Justice shall have full jurisdiction within the meaning of Article 172 of the Treaty to adjudicate on proceedings instituted against the decisions by which the Commission has fixed a fine or a penalty; it may cancel, reduce or increase the fine or the penalty imposed.

Article 18

Unit of account

For the purposes of Articles 15 to 17 the unit of account shall be that adopted for drawing up the budget of the Community in accordance with Articles 207 and 209 of the Treaty.

Article 19

Hearing of the parties concerned and of third parties

1. Before taking decisions as provided for in Articles 2, 3, 6, 7, 8, 15 and 16, the Commission shall give the enterprises or associations of enterprises concerned an opportunity to express their views on the points

objected to which have been taken into consideration by the Commission.
2. So far as the Commission or the competent authorities of the Member States consider it necessary, they may also hear other natural or legal persons or associations of persons. If natural or legal persons or associations of persons who show that they have a sufficient interest ask to be heard, ther request shall be granted.
3. When the Commission intends to give negative clearance pursuant to Article 2 or to issue a declaration under Article 85, paragraph 3, of the Treaty, it shall publish the essential content of the application or notification, inviting all interested third parties to submit their observations within a time-limit which it shall fix and which shall not be less than one month. Publication shall respect the justified interest of enterprises that their business secrets should not be divulged.

Article 20

Professional secrets

1. Information gathered pursuant to Articles 11, 12, 13 and 14 may not be used for any purpose other than that for which it was requested.
2. Without prejudice to the provisions of Articles 19 and 21, the Commission and the competent authorities of the Member States as well as their officials and other employees may not disclose matters which have come to their knowledge through the application of the present Regulation and which by their nature are professional secrets.
3. The provisions of paragraphs 1 and 2 shall not hinder the publication of general surveys or reviews not containing information relating to particular enterprises or associations of enterprises.

Article 21

Publication of decisions

1. The Commission shall publish the decisions which it takes pursuant to Articles 2, 3, 6, 7 and 8.
2. The publication shall name the parties concerned and give the essential content of the decisions; the justified interest of the enterprises that their business secrets should not be divulged shall be respected.

Article 22

Special Provisions

1. The Commission shall submit to the Council proposals for making certain categories of agreements, decisions and concerted practices such as are referred to in Article 4, paragraph 2, and Article 5, paragraph 2, subject to the notification provided for in Articles 4 and 5.
2. Within one year from the entry into force of the present Regulation the Council shall examine, on a proposal of the Commission, any special provisions which could be made in derogation from the provisions

contained in this Regulation with respect to the agreements, decisions and concerted practices referred to in Article 4, paragraph 2, and Article 5, paragraph 2.

Article 23

Transitional system applicable to decisions taken by authorities of Member States

1. Agreements, decisions and concerted practices referred to in Article 85, paragraph 1, of the Treaty to which, before the entry into force of this Regulation, the competent authority of a Member State has declared Article 85, paragraph 1, to be inapplicable pursuant to Article 85, paragraph 3, shall not be subject to the notification provided for in Article 5. The decision of the competent authority of the Member State shall be considered a decision within the meaning of Article 6; its validity shall expire at the latest on the date which the said authority has fixed, but may not exceed a duration of three years reckoned from the entry into force of the present Regulation. Article 8, paragraph 3 shall apply.
2. Applications for renewal of the decisions referred to in paragraph 1 shall be settled by the Commission in accordance with Article 8, paragraph 2.

Article 24

Implementing provisions

The Commission shall have authority to lay down implementing provisions concerning the form, content and other details of applications submitted pursuant to Articles 2 and 3 and of the notification provided for in Articles 4 and 5, and to lay down those concerning the hearings provided for in Article 19, paragraphs 1 and 2.

The present Regulation shall be binding in every respect and directly applicable in each Member State.

Done at Brussels, 6 February 1962
By the Council
The President
M. COUVE DE MURVILLE

ARTICLES OF THE E.E.C. TREATY CITED IN THE TEXT

INDEX

UNIVERSITY LIBRARY NOTTINGHAM